A WING
AND A
PRAYER

*Defined Contribution
Plans and the
Pursuit of 24 Karat
Golden Years*

INVESTORS
PRESS

Published in the United States by Investors Press.

Library of Congress Cataloging-in-Publication Data
    Investors Press
    A Wing and a Prayer: Defined Contribution Plans and the Pursuit of 24 Karat
                Golden Years/Investors Press
      ISBN 1-885123-01-9
      I. A Wing and a Prayer:
          Defined Contribution Plans and the Pursuit of 24 Karat Golden Years
Printed in Mexico

10 9   8   7   6   5   4   3   2   1

Jacket art and design © 1994 by Wendell Minor
Book design by Silver Communications Inc.
Corporate & Consultant Edition

ACKNOWLEDGEMENT

*I*nvestors Press is pleased to present **A Wing and a Prayer**, the second of four books in its 1994 Investment Management Series.

Each of these original books examines issues of compelling concern to pension and investment officers, trustees, benefits administrators, pensions consultants and money managers. Each book is written by distinguished professionals in the field whose essays reflect their own independent and informed opinions.

Edited and published by Investors Press, this unique educational Series is made possible through the underwriting of a small group of leading firms to whom appreciation goes from everyone who values the importance of education and the candid exchange of information. Because of their vision and commitment, this new Series becomes a tool for the sharing of experience and insight and initiates an essential bridge between members of the investment community that encourages dialogue, discussion and deeper understanding.

INVESTORS
PRESS

1994 INVESTMENT MANAGEMENT BOOK SERIES

Underwritten by

ANGELO, GORDON & CO.

BARINGS

CHANCELLOR CAPITAL MANAGEMENT

DELAWARE MANAGEMENT COMPANY, INC.

THE DREYFUS TRUST COMPANY

FIDELITY INVESTMENTS

INSTINET

MELLON TRUST

METLIFE

MERRILL LYNCH

NCM CAPITAL

TABLE OF CONTENTS

INTRODUCTION

*F*ew issues today have a more powerful personal immediacy for American employees than the often confusing, but always daunting, planning required to ensure a comfortable, safe and secure retirement. Beyond compensation and health care benefits during working years, anticipation of future needs weighs heavily on both employees and their employers. Vast numbers of people are only beginning to grasp the enormity of this problem: even mid-level employees must have nearly seven-figure nest eggs to ensure a modest standard of living during retirement. Increasingly, as Defined Contribution (DC) plans augment and replace Defined Benefits (DB) plans as the primary source of retirement income and the DOL's 404(c) regulations redefine employer obligations, the complex world of retirement planning, participant responsibility and fiduciary obligation requires urgent clarification.

Employers must acknowledge and accept their responsibility to decide and describe clearly the extent of their retirement commitment to their workforce; employee expectations can be met only when they are understood. And employees, increasingly empowered by their growing participation in the decisions that will mold and shape their retirement outcome, must accept responsibility for asking questions, learning from available educational tools, weighing risks and making informed choices that are in their best personal long-term interests.

As historical relationships continue to shift between employer and employed, and the shape of career structures — length, loyalty, location — reconfigures to reflect the pressures and possibilities of an ongoing technological revolution, new definitions of institutional and individual responsibility emerge. The issues examined in **A Wing and A Prayer: *Defined Contribution Plans and the Pursuit of 24 Karat Golden Years*** consider fundamental, as well as specific, challenges facing plan sponsors as they meet their fiduciary responsibilities.

The stunning growth of the DC industry, with its dizzying array of products and services, and the tidal shift of retirement planning responsibility from plan sponsor to plan participant make starting or changing a plan a fearsome task, especially for benefits managers who, unlike their counterparts on the DC side, often have little or no investment experience.

Buffeted by such rapid growth, the government has struggled to analyze and understand DC plan trends and establish new requirements that protect workers' benefits and describe employers' obligations. Many sponsors, however, believe the 404(c) regulations stipulating baseline requirements are far too minimal and their description of fiduciary protection ambiguous. Beyond the moral dilemma of "doing the right thing," companies face the overwhelming obstacles of understanding their legal obligations and protecting themselves from liability for participant investment losses. Given America's labor history of employee/management legal confrontation, such concern is justifiable. The need for clear, understandable information shared between the government, plan sponsor and plan participant is paramount.

As DC plans differ fundamentally from DB plans (which focus on company contribution levels and time-tested actuarial assumptions), they must consider more qualitative, subjective "cultural" issues: the specifics of each company's employee base. While few states or municipalities have made DC plans their core benefit plan, more are studying the possibility seriously. Chronic deficits, ballooning benefit obligations and decreased investment returns all underscore this need for alternatives. In the government sector DC plans are already growing as supplemental benefits.

Adding to the myriad of choices, 457 plans (supplementary deferred compensation) were offered by 46 states and more than 50 municipalities as recently as June 1993. Although they are much less attractive to employees than DC plans and do not offer similar protection, the same principles of separate account investing apply. Congress may soon reinstate the 401(k) for public entities, rescinded in 1986. If 401(k)s are reinstated, it is likely they will attract more participant assets than 457's and push themselves even more into the public view.

Although fiduciary responsibilities required of ERISA plans may not apply to public funds, the ethical obligation to educate and inform, while not overstepping the line into advising, remains. The practical considerations of funding and potential liability are, ultimately, common to all plan alternatives, as is responsibility to the growing number of retirees who remain active plan participants and must be considered as well.

As sponsors fulfill their fiduciary responsibilities by structuring plans with investment options that meet the needs of their particular employee base, and participants learn how to use available information to make individual choices, a single reality emerges with powerful clarity: there is no consensus on the interpretation of 404(c) compliance and protection; confusion persists and clarity may emerge only over time as specific cases are tested in the courts. The result: companies are blazing their own trails in establishing or refining their plans. As our distinguished authors demonstrate, everyone is writing his own book.

Nathaniel H. Duffield, *Director, Trust Investments, Halliburton Company* recounts the fascinating history and evolution of his company's long-established and uniquely structured DC plan in his chapter "The Best of Both Worlds: Applying DB Principles to Your DC Plan." Using the lessons of its half-century of experience and success, Duffield underscores the importance of a strong team working toward clear and obtainable goals of long-term growth, effective cost management and ongoing, consistent communication and education with participants. He encourages building long-term relationships with outside managers chosen after extensive due diligence and suggests giving participants flexibility in investment options, but not too much — since too many options often add nothing more than confusion and trendy new products may lack real relevance for your company.

Sally Gottlieb, *Benefits Manager, Apple Computer* candidly reveals in "Truth or Consequences in DC Plan Management" that her company's DC plan will not meet the total retirement needs of all its employees. Few companies take as direct an approach as Apple does: it identifies the shortfall looming on the retirement horizon and actively pursues a communication/education program intended to prepare, inform and educate its workforce. Using traditional tools (print media, focus groups, surveys) in combination with innovative forms of presentation and new high-tech aids (modeling, self-paced interactive software) Apple is committed to understanding the needs of its employees, structuring its plan to meet those needs and delivering key messages that help plan participants use their increased investment responsibility wisely. The company's overall philosophy is centered on an honest dialogue with its employees; the specifics of its plan structure reflect its willingness to deal honestly with the possibilities and limitations of its plan.

Rita Metras, *Director, Employee Benefits – Retirement and Savings Plans, Eastman Kodak Company* outlines "A Back To Basics Guide for Your DC Plan" in her chapter on implementing or changing a DC plan. Drawing on her experience with the Kodak fund's $3 billion asset base, she highlights potential hazards and emphasizes the need to crystallize company goals and objectives as you structure investment options. Utilizing the knowledge and expertise of a complete team, she urges companies to formulate their position on 404(c) compliance, develop an adequate education/communication program and invite maximum employee input. Metras reminds readers to assess and understand costs, examine volatility and gather intelligence on the merits of different options, products, and services from practitioners, industry associations and providers. Plan sponsors who consider expanding their plan options in anticipation of continually changing interest rates will find much of interest and value in Metras' discussion of which investment options realistically benefit different groups of employees.

In addition to the important insights and guidance shared by our authors, Investors Press includes a **Special 404(c) Report** intended to help readers cut through the continuing confusion that clouds the interpretation of this regulation; honors one of a new breed of emerging DC industry Trailblazers and features an innovative Resource Guide designed to increase the book's usefulness and reference value.

A Wing and A Prayer, the second book in our 1994 Investment Management Series, continues the standard of excellence, clarity and candor established by our inaugural book, **The Changing Face of Pension Management,** which the entire Series, an important and innovative educational project, will meet.

Joan Kaplan
Executive Editor
Investors Press
Washington, Connecticut

Rocky Road or Plain Vanilla:
A Back To Basics Guide For Your DC Plan

Rita D. Metras

Your organization, like many others today, may be implementing or consider-ing important changes in its defined contribution (DC) plan. The urgent need to reevaluate and restructure existing plans reflects the dramatically increased pressure on our plan sponsor community to meet changing retirement needs and expectations.

Does any of this sound familiar?

➤ Your existing funds have turned in a poor or unsatisfactory performance.

➤ Your participants are expressing increased interest in more investment options and they want more convenient transfer options (daily valuation or a quicker turnaround on loans).

➤ Management pressure within your organization is increasing. Fiscal pressures, staff reductions, and the extra burdens of compliance with government regulations are forcing you to outsource all or some benefit functions. You must consider cost-shifting plan expenses to plan partici-pants as another alternative to reduce your plan's operating costs.

➤ You don't currently offer at least three investment options and are con-sidering expanding your offerings, if only to comply with ERISA Section 404(c), a voluntary rule that offers plan sponsors at least limited protec-tion from potential liability. (See **Special 404(c) Report**.)

1. What Are Your Plan's Objectives?

Whatever the specific triggering factors, plan sponsors must have a clear idea of their objectives before implementing new, or modifying existing, savings/retire-ment plans. This warning may seem obvious, but acceding to pressures for change without fully assessing and understanding your goals and the consequences of change is ultimately counter-productive. By considering the following five factors and their relevance to your company's unique circumstances, you should be better equipped to make more informed and appropriate decisions that can benefit both your organization and its employees.

1. **Employee Participation:** What percentage of your employees currently participates in your plan? What level of participation do you consider desirable? Does your management agree? If not, how do you reconcile these differences? Do you understand why participation is lower than desired? Do you know who is not participating and why? Do you periodically survey employees to try to better understand their resistance points as you develop a more responsive strategy? Would offering additional alternative investment options, or a company match, help boost participation to desired levels? Would more educational information provide a key ingredient for a more successful overall plan program and fuller participation?

2. **Educating the Plan Participants:** How well do your participants understand their investment options? Do they have a working knowledge of basic investment concepts: compound interest, risk and return, the impact of inflation on fixed income investments, how interest rate movements affect bond prices? If participants don't have a solid, working understanding of their current investment options, your communication/information/education efforts may need beefing up. Experience has taught us that offerings of new alternative investments require even more thorough explanation.[1]

3. **Asset Base:** What is the size of your current asset base? Will new investment options attract additional money and investment participation, or will existing money simply be reallocated? What is the minimum level of contributions you expect a new fund to attract (either in dollars or as a percentage of assets) in order to justify its addition as an investment option?

4. **Investment Options:** Are you satisfied with the plan's current investment options, or do you feel the need for more diversity? What percentage of assets does each option attract? Does each fund's historical long-term performance justify retaining it? Is your company stock included in available options? Do you want to encourage shifts in investment away from more conservative funds and GICs to more aggressive funds? Do you have, as Kodak does, a "stepping-stone"[2] fund to attract potential investors who have not yet invested in a stock fund?

5. **404(c) Compliance:** The "broad range" of investments called for in Section 404(c) is defined as at least three core investment alternatives, not including company stock, which have materially different risk/return characteristics.

Plan sponsors who comply with all the provisions of 404(c) can expect protection from liability for losses that result from a participant's investment decisions. But there are no safe harbors, no absolute guarantees and no preset combinations of

---

[1] See **Filling the Vacuum:** *Alternative Investments for Pension Plans, Endowments and Foundations*, Investors Press, 1994.

[2] "Stepping-stone" is a term I use to describe a balanced fund that combines bonds with some equities to give participants a modest degree of equity exposure as an introduction to equities.

investment options that qualify for absolute protection. Nor does 404(c) protect fiduciaries from lawsuits based on the selection of investments or investment managers.

The regulation requires that participants must also be given "independent control" of their participation: they must be able to transfer among investment alternatives with a frequency appropriate to the expected volatility of the investment, but not less often than once every three months. They must have reasonable opportunity to give investment instructions, receive written confirmations, and be free from improper influence in any of these decisions from a plan fiduciary or plan sponsor.

Many DC sponsors already fulfill all or most of the minimum requirements. If your company is near compliance, what remaining steps need to be taken to comply fully?

2. THE DC TEAM

If your company offers a Defined Benefit (DB) plan, it is reasonable for the Employee Benefits or DC administrator to expect assistance from the DB investment director. Since the Human Resources department of your company probably handles your communications/education program, it is important that they be involved from the outset. Counsel must also review any changes in the existing plan to ensure that legal and fiduciary requirements are fulfilled. If plan administration is handled internally, you will need to involve those responsible to ensure that any proposed investment options meet all valuation and administrative requirements.

Keep in mind that if you decide to offer a combination of funds from different vendors, or certain types of institutional funds (see Beyond Mutual Funds), valuation is often more difficult than it is with a single mutual fund supplier. Make sure that the funds you select fit your valuation cycle. Be sure they meet your administrative

YOUR 404(C) COMMUNICATIONS CHECKLIST[3]

Section 404(c) stipulates a number of communications requirements:

✓ Participants must be notified that the plan intends to comply with 404(c), and what protection it grants to the plan sponsor.

✓ A description of all investment alternatives is required.

✓ Investment managers must be identified.

✓ An explanation of how participants can give their investment instruction, and any restrictions that apply, must be given.

✓ A description of transaction fees and expenses such as commissions, sales loads or redemption fees must be given.

✓ Participants must receive details on confidentiality of transactions and voting rights if company stock is an option.

✓ Copies of the most recent prospectuses sent to the plan for investments subject to the Securities Act of 1933 must be provided to plan participants before or after each initial investment is made.[4]

✓ Identification of the plan fiduciary who will provide additional information "on request" must be made.

---

[3] This list is intended as a guideline and highlights only key requirements. Consult with your legal counsel for complete requirements. See **Special 404(c) Report** for additional information.

[4] The regulation doesn't specify what kind of information document, if any, it requires for investment options other than mutual funds or company stock.

processing requirements. If you have an unbundled arrangement, check carefully in advance with your trustee to identify potential problems.

3. The Importance of Employee Input

Fund selection and structure involve more than just picking the best possible investments. You must also consider the level of employee interest and knowledge. If you offer investments that employees don't understand or aren't interested in, you've wasted your time and their opportunity.

Unless you already provide ample communications, most of your plan participants probably know little about retirement investing. As a result, many employees invest wholly, or substantially, in conservative options because they are often the most understandable and appear to be the "safest." Not only is it critically important to offer a range of funds that are made understandable to the average employee, investment education efforts must explain the importance of diversifying one's retirement portfolio.

> ➤ If employees don't understand an investment option, they will mistrust it and often avoid it altogether. Participants will not put their money into something they don't understand or trust. Would you?

> ➤ Participants need to know that their input is important and that they are being heard. By soliciting their input, you not only encourage more learning and more active participation, you collect valuable information that helps you develop more responsive and productive plan programs.

Survey questions might range from such basics as "If an XYZ fund were available, would you invest in it?" to issues of risk tolerance and plan design. At Kodak, for instance, we asked employees how well they understood our proposed options and how important "name recognition" was for them when they choose an investment fund. We even asked our employees how the investment options should be named.

Xerox Corporation surveyed 9,500 of its 55,000 employees in 1992 before expanding its DC investment options. According to Paul Rivera, Manager, Benefits Planning and Operations, Xerox gave survey participants a hypothetical sum of money to "invest," along with a description of the available funds. The company then monitored the results of the employee allocations and made subsequent decisions regarding investment options that were more relevant to its workforce.

Employee focus groups are often even more revealing than survey results, although much more costly to conduct. Responses to questions are usually better understood since you can take the time to explain options in detail and clarify any confusing points during the discussion. There is also, obviously, more opportunity for qualitative and anecdotal input. It is often wise to hire an experienced consultant to run a focus group or to develop actionable information beyond the most basic surveys. The cost and the time commitment to obtain the most accurate employee input can be considerable, but it is usually an investment that yields great returns in the long run.

4. BUNDLED, UNBUNDLED OR ALLIANCE ARRANGEMENTS: WHICH BEST MEETS YOUR NEEDS?

Bundled: Typically, a bundled arrangement provides trustee services including recordkeeping, administration and a telephone center along with investment services. Many vendors also include additional explanatory investment communications as part of their package. Net costs to the company should be lower because management fees and other fund operating expenses (paid by participants) can offset a good portion of the recordkeeping costs. One clear advantage to the participants in a bundled arrangement is "one-stop" shopping.

On the downside, however, certain services, particularly recordkeeping, are often less flexible than they are in unbundled arrangements. Furthermore, if the relationship sours or you become dissatisfied with one aspect of service, you may have to disrupt other aspects of the plan which are working well.

Unbundled: In an unbundled arrangement, the plan sponsor contracts separately for investment and trustee services, ideally choosing the best, most cost-effective providers for each service. Each company must evaluate the pluses and minuses of this approach based on its own needs.

Alliances: Alliances offer more flexibility than bundled services, often at less cost than unbundled arrangements, and with the added benefit of an intermediary and ally. With an alliance, the consulting firm is your core contact. It not only oversees the recordkeeping and operates the phone center, it arranges for a trustee and organizes a package of several investment options from many investment firms. Communication packages can be included and, if there are numerous choices, some consultants will also assist with investment selection. If a particular investment option or mutual fund is not offered through the alliance, the consultant will generally try to add it.

5. COST

When you evaluate fees, assume that participants are paying all the fees and then look at total costs. It is extremely difficult to get an apples-to-apples comparison because of the way fees are quoted, and few investment options are similar enough to make valid comparisons.

As a hypothetical comparison, consider one common investment option, an index fund based on the S&P 500 Index, where in every case the performance would be nearly equal before fees. On a $50 million S&P Index fund fees could range from 9 basis points (100 basis points equal 1%) if purchased as a stand-alone, to 18 basis points as in the case of an alliance (10 of which might later be credited to offset other costs), to 28 basis points as part of a bundled arrangement. In this example, the spread of 21 basis points alone is equivalent to $105,000 in reduced returns. Keep in mind, however, that this bundled fee would cover comprehensive, state-of-the-art services such as daily valuation, newspaper listings and voice confirmation.

Consider the costs from the plan sponsor's perspective. In many bundled arrangements, expenses such as recordkeeping can be significantly reduced when the vendor takes into account investment dollars that will be invested in the products offered by the investment manager. When considering bundled

Few investment firms are more trusted by more people than Merrill Lynch. Perhaps that's because for over 100 years, our focus has always been on our clients' best interests.

THE DIFFERENCE
BETWEEN "TRUST ME"
AND TRUST

Markets go up. Markets go down.

When the market goes into a correction, you're getting calls from your employees wanting to know if their investments are safe.

You're getting calls from top management wanting to know if your 401(k) provider is not only available to take your calls, but that they're still in business.

Many 401(k) providers simply can't cut it in a steep correction. Not so with Merrill Lynch.

Maybe it's because we're the best capitalized firm in the business. Maybe it's because we're more than stable.

We're committed to the individuals who have their 401(k) assets with us. Plan Sponsors and their employees trust us and we work hard to keep that trust.

Individuals are why we work hard to keep our fund performance at top caliber and our firm in strong financial shape.

And people like you are why we work for a paperless environment to make your administration easier.

Education is key. We teach the realities of retirement.

We distribute educational materials including custom videotapes, retirement planning diskettes, and multimedia kiosks.

We also offer daily valuation and financial modeling on a toll-free number.

We're individuals at Merrill Lynch. And we serve companies and individuals the best way we know how—one by one.

We're there for them. Good times and bad. We think that makes a difference.

For more information, please call Donna Winn, Vice President, at 609-282-2233.

The difference is Merrill Lynch.

 **Merrill Lynch**
A tradition of trust.

arrangements, be sure you understand the charges for investments outside the family of funds offered by the investment manager. These fees often depend on the value of the relationship, but could vary from 5 to 20 basis points on the assets in the non-family funds.

In alliance arrangements there are usually no additional charges for outside funds, but there are also no fee offsets available to those funds. With alliance investments, the plan sponsor receives a "rebate" of a portion of the fund's operating expenses, based on either the number of participants or on a specified percentage of the assets under management. These "rebated" amounts can be used to reduce the recordkeeping and phone center costs to the plan sponsor to make them more comparable to those of bundled arrangements.

Commissions on sales of company stock as well as management fees on GICs can vary widely depending on the arrangement and the investment manager. Costs paid by the plan or imbedded in the fund ultimately reduce the participants' return; it is essential to know and understand just what all the charges are.

6. HOW MANY INVESTMENT OPTIONS SHOULD YOU OFFER?

Is there an optimal number of funds to offer in your DC plan?[5] What is right for another company's employee base may not be right for yours. Indeed, as your participants become increasingly comfortable with your DC plan, your own optimal number may change. One thing remains certain: how many options to offer is a subject of growing debate, particularly since the 404(c) rules went into effect.

The pressure for companies to "keep up with the Joneses" and remain competitive in benefits within their industry is part of the reason sponsors are adding more fund options. Some sponsors say their employees simply feel "more is better." But concern about 404(c) compliance is another important part as well. Right or wrong, some sponsors still feel that the more fund choices, the greater their protection under 404(c).

Many investment managers and consultants heartily disagree, and consider it a disservice to offer plan participants 20 or 30 investment options, as a few companies do. Too many choices can overwhelm and confuse participants, especially when the distinctions between similar funds become blurred or too arcane to articulate understandably to participants. Most practitioners feel that adequate diversification can easily be achieved with well under ten funds.

For an early stage plan, I believe that six funds, excluding a company stock fund, is a workable minimum to adequately cover the risk/return spectrum. Unless the majority of your participant pool is highly educated, or participants are already

---

[5] When it comes to a "magic number" of investment option choices, there is simply no overwhelming consensus. According to the Profit Sharing Council of America (36th Annual Survey of Profit Sharing and 401(k) Plans, 1993, p. 16), 39% of all plans surveyed offered five or more fund options. There appear to be few broadbased surveys of employee preferences. In 1992, the Frank Russell Company published a survey of plan participants selected from a cross-section of 500 companies. Participants were asked how many options they preferred. Over 70% wanted between three and five options; almost 20% wanted six or more. More than half of all respondents felt it was "very important" to have more than three investment choices, although the number dropped substantially when the scenario involved participants' paying the fee. ("Retirement Planning in America," Frank Russell Company, 1992, pp. 13-14.)

comfortable with the plan, more than four funds may be pushing the limits of participant understanding.

Is there any harm, other than obfuscation, in offering too many options? Depending on your fee arrangement, recordkeeping costs could be too costly to justify many additional options, especially if they attract few assets. Since the plan sponsor has to provide communications for every fund option, the cost/benefit ratio to produce and distribute materials to your total participant pool for a fund with minimal participation might not be practical.

From my experience with the Kodak fund's asset base of $3 billion, I feel an investment option should attract at least 5% of total participant assets to justify its existence. How long should you allow for a new fund to gain use? Three years is reasonable, with steady asset growth year by year.

7. Asset Classes

You must be absolutely sure that your plan participants will be offered a fund or combination of funds that will meet the risk/return objectives of their individual circumstances.

To encourage participation, there is sometimes no substitute for name recognition. A well-known, high-performance fund will often attract participant dollars. In addition, if your goal is to encourage employees to shift assets from fixed-income or other "conservative" investments, equity and other funds with name recognition may provide just the incentive. In any case, whether "name brand" or "private label," investment options must be both distinct and understandable. Communications must be clear.

Once you get beyond the bread and butter offerings (common stock, broad index funds, balanced funds), how do you choose among particular management styles? If you want to keep your offerings to a reasonable number, how do you decide whether a small-cap equity fund, as an example, is preferable to a value or growth fund?

One way to help provide a meaningful range of options for plan participants is to choose them according to how closely they correlate to the stock market. R^2 is a mathematical measure of this correlation. An R^2 of 1.0, like that of the S&P 500 Index, indicates a perfect performance correlation to the market, while an R^2 of zero represents complete independence from the market. We would expect that an actively managed bond fund, an international securities fund or a precious metals fund would have a low R^2.

If you are considering offering anything beyond three or four "plain vanilla" options in your DC plan, R^2 can help you be sure your offerings provide your participants with sufficient diversification. You should look for funds with different R^2 correlations to ensure they will not all go up or down at the same time and will offer different risk/reward characteristics that meet the varying objectives of your participants.

"Tilt" funds can also be used to achieve greater diversification while maintaining a manageable number of fund options. Rather than offer a separate growth stock fund, for instance, you could offer an equity fund that is 60% weighted or "tilted" toward growth stocks to provide growth returns.

8. Individual Securities: Pros and Cons

Have you considered allowing the purchase of individual securities as part of your plan's investment options? Currently, few plan sponsors offer this option, and when offered, it often draws only negligible numbers of their participants. Most often they are participants who have higher account balances and want to exercise more control over their holdings.

Although interest in this type of option is growing slowly, administrative and cost obstacles persist. Technological advances may bring costs down, but plan sponsors must address and meet the more complex communications and fiduciary challenges they present.

9. The Mutual Fund Window: A Simple Way to Offer More Choices

How can plan sponsors offer more participant choice without going to individual securities or having so many investment options that participants are overwhelmed? A "mutual fund window" is one solution. It allows "off-the-menu" choices for those interested in more than standard options, without committing time and expense to adding and testing new options for all participants.

Participants can choose from among a specified number of funds through a mutual fund family outside the core options. If the window provider differs from the core fund provider, window options investment activity won't appear on participants' statements from your recordkeeper; only their dollar investment will show up. Detailed fund activity comes directly from the mutual fund company itself.

The cost for window options varies, depending on many factors: the scope of the option, whether you offer participants windows with other fund vendors, and the size of assets under management. Windows raise recordkeeping costs because

they require special arrangements between fund manager and recordkeeper. As with any fund feature, regardless of who pays, sponsors must consider the expected participation levels and the resulting cost/benefit ratio of any special arrangements. Remember, it is still unclear how detailed communications need to be for window funds, or how frequently they need to be updated.

The window concept is relatively new and few companies currently offer this feature. It is one shortcut to offering funds outside the core funds and a feature that is gaining ground. Not only does it give participants added flexibility, some plan sponsors see it as extra insurance against 404(c) liability. [6]

10. PRE-PACKAGED ALLOCATIONS

"Lifecycle" funds, alternatively known as "lifestyle" or "risk profile" funds, have been growing in popularity. These funds consist of a predetermined mix of two or more asset classes that meet certain objectives and correspond to the risk profile of a particular phase or life cycle of the employee. Most commonly, they are composed of commingled funds or mutual funds, although individual securities or even a combination of other funds can be included in the lifecycle fund.

Since many participants do not understand the principles of diversification — or how their individual investment risk profile changes over the course of their working lifetime — pre-packaged allocations eliminate the need for participants to make asset allocation decisions. The sponsor offers a "Chinese menu" of lifecycle fund choices, each designed specifically to meet the needs of a given risk profile. Participants simply select the fund(s) that currently best meet their needs and

---

[6] It should be noted that 404(c) does not require offering more than three funds with different risk/return characteristics. The idea of "extra insurance" is, therefore, an unnecessary, if reassuring, step sponsors can take.

through the communications program they are reminded to move to a fund or funds with decreased risk as they enter each new "lifecycle."

A newer variation of this concept is even more automatic. Participants can select one or more of five funds based on their own projected horizon date (usually their year of retirement) and stay with that fund for their entire career. The fund's level of risk, keyed to the needs of specific demographic groups, changes automatically for each risk profile without requiring participants to move assets themselves as they change brackets.[7] The only decision the participant need ever make is how much money to put into the fund(s).

The whole concept of lifecycle funds remains controversial, particularly this new variation, because, critics claim, plan sponsor liability under 404(c) is unclear. Since the plan sponsor provides options with built-in risk tolerance levels and eliminates participant risk choices, lifecycle funds could be construed as offering investment advice. For the automatic package of funds, the concern is magnified: if participants need never again think about their fund after making the initial selection and if, over time, the fund's performance is disappointing, some believe there could be additional liability for the plan sponsor.

11. BEYOND MUTUAL FUNDS

Many companies that are expanding their investments look only at mutual funds. There are other important options, however, such as institutional commingled funds, or separate accounts, which can be tailored for your specific plan.

Fees for institutional commingled funds can be *significantly less* than those for mutual funds. Although prices are not listed in the newspapers for these funds, the recordkeeper could still provide an 800 number for participant inquiries. If daily valuation is a feature you want to provide, be aware that some excellent institutional funds do not yet offer this capability.

Separate accounts, often dedicated exclusively to an individual company's participant assets, offer many of the advantages of DB plans, most notably interaction between plan sponsor and investment manager.[8]

12. SHOULD YOU USE A CONSULTANT?

You don't need the help or expense of an outside consultant if you have all the in-house expertise and resources necessary to research your options, make your choices and hire and monitor your service providers.

But, if your in-house capabilities are limited, outside consultants can offer valuable help in all aspects of the investment process, from assisting with the development of an investment policy to determining types of funds to be offered and selecting the fund managers. Consultants can also develop employee surveys, run employee focus groups and provide employee communications. They can provide useful information on what their other plan sponsor clients are doing as well. This can include sharing with you examples of effective communications materials used by other plans.

---

[7] See discussion of lifecycle funds and 404(c) in **Special 404(c) Report**.
[8] For a thorough discussion of separate accounts, see Nathaniel H. Duffield's chapter "The Best of Both Worlds: Applying DB Principles to Your DC Plan."

Imagine this:

You're reallocating equity assets: selling Japan, Malaysia and Hong Kong; buying the U.K., Holland and Finland. You need it done

[direct, local access in over 30 countries]

today–100% completion. What's more, three of the orders represent more than two

[the difficult trades]

days' average volume. You need to protect your profile, and you need local liquidity

[anonymity reduces market impact]

and best execution in all six markets–now. How are you going to do this? There's only

[a complete transaction analysis service]

one choice: access order flow directly and reach local brokers and exchanges, global

[the neutrality of a global agency broker]

institutions and wholesalers all at the same time. To complete the trades, balance

[instant, simultaneous communication]

the cash, receive more trading information and fulfill some research commitments–

[a worldwide soft commission capability]

You're going to Instinet.

[for information call 800-225-5008]

This is trading.

INSTIN T.
A REUTER COMPANY

Instinet clients. Focused on performance.

When hiring outside consultants for any part of the process, be aware of potential conflicts of interest that can arise from their business relationships associated with such services as "manager of managers" funds or recordkeeping. Relationship ties like these are a fact of life in the consulting world today and are increasingly common.[9] Most consultants reassure us that they do not practice favoritism (long-term, it would hardly seem to be in their best interest to do so), but you must be aware of this potential bias and avoid any conflict of interest.

13. CHOOSING YOUR MANAGERS

At the very least, you must exercise standard due diligence. Examine the performance record (long-term performance across the range of investment options being offered to evaluate continuity in investment strategy and style), fees, staffing, turnover, research capability; how the firm selects and monitors funds; and then gauge the manager's understanding of your plan and the needs of your participants.

The manager's history is important, yet it is often overlooked as a criterion for selection by DC plan sponsors. To the extent that it can and does affect performance and rates of return, stability of personnel is also important. If one portfolio manager has primary investment responsibility for a fund, be sure to find out what fund that person managed previously and check its performance under his or her watch. Are other portfolio managers qualified to step in if that manager leaves?

High personnel turnover may signal a problem. If the investment personnel remain within the firm to manage other investments, however, this might only mean that the investment process depends more on teamwork, or a computer model, than on the stewardship of an individual portfolio manager. The basis of the manager's compensation could also a problem. Is it based on the total fund or fund family performance, or is the manager rewarded only for performance of the part of the fund he or she is managing?

14. MANAGEMENT FEES & FUND OPERATING EXPENSES: BOTTOM LINE IMPACT

Because fiduciaries are required to ensure that expenses charged to the plan are reasonable, it is critical that you have a clear and thorough understanding of the management fees and any other expenses for which your fund is charged. Returns should, of course, always be analyzed *net of fees and operating expenses.*

15. SELECTING INVESTMENT OPTIONS: LOOKING AT HISTORICAL RETURNS

Performance is often reported in only one, three, five, and sometimes, ten-year increments. If all you look at is aggregate returns, you miss getting valuable information by comparing the ups and downs against benchmarks. On the down-side, this practice can give undue weight to a very good or a very bad year and can frequently mask the volatility of the fund. As an example, the one, three, five and

---

[9] See **The Changing Face of Pension Management: Rescripting the Role of Plan Sponsors, Trustees, Money Managers and Consultants**, Investors Press, 1994.

ten-year returns of the S&P 500 through December 1993 were 10.1, 15.6, 14.5 and 14.9%, respectively. What these numbers don't show, however, is that in 1990 there was a negative return of –3.3%, and that in 1985, 1989, and 1991 the returns topped 30%!

Look at the yearly return of a fund against its benchmark. At the least, you should watch closely to see if a fund underperforms significantly against its benchmark in down markets. And certainly, if a fund has a negative performance when the benchmark is positive, the fund manager had better have a reasonable and acceptable explanation.

16. RISK: IS YOUR MANAGER DELIVERING ENOUGH ALPHA?

Another significant factor in choosing investments is the amount of each fund's risk or volatility. Risk is really just another way of expressing volatility. It is important to make sure that there is ample differentiation among your funds along the risk spectrum.

One way to measure volatility is standard deviation, the dispersion of the rates of return around the arithmetic mean. Higher deviation indicates greater variance of returns against the average, and thus, greater risk. To measure the volatility of a fund relative to the S&P 500, use the beta coefficient. A fund with a beta of 1.00 has the same volatility as the market; one with a beta greater than 1.00 is more volatile than the market, less than 1.00 is less volatile than the market.

What if a fund goes up or down more than is expected by its beta coefficient? That difference, known as the alpha, is a measure of the fund's superior, or inferior, performance. *What value added or incremental alpha does your manager provide?* Many DC plan sponsors tend to overlook alpha, but they shouldn't: it isolates and identifies the success or failure of the manager's expertise, reflecting the extent to which good or bad performance is the result of his or her management beyond market conditions. Isn't this what you are paying your manager to deliver?

It may be misleading to look at absolute return. You need to consider the *risk-adjusted return*. Over the past decade, the markets have heavily favored more aggressive managers. But in a down market, volatility will hurt, rather than reward, these managers.

Beyond volatility is the longer-term risk of inflation. Many participants perceive a heavy weighting in fixed income investments such as GICs to be "safer," but they are overlooking the erosion of return over time caused by inflation. Communications programs must address not only the characteristics of each fund and the importance of diversification, but the root, underlying principles including various forms of investment, market and inflation risk.

17. A WORD OF CAUTION

Although do-it-yourself investment option selection is certainly possible, it is not advisable for everyone, especially the neophyte investor. Remember your fiduciary responsibility as a "prudent man." You might ask, "If I pick good funds, what's the problem?" There isn't one — until the performance of the fund falters or there is a serious problem with the underlying assets of an investment, or participants decide it's your fault if they are losing money. Your selection process must withstand extreme scrutiny. That's why sound advice from experienced, proven professionals is a good move, both for you and your plan participants. You are also responsible for monitoring your funds' performance regularly to ensure that they are performing acceptably.

It is critical that plan participants be given investment options that take into account the long-term nature of retirement savings. Without proper diversification, and with too conservative a posture early on, participants' ability to retire in comfort, as they expect, may indeed be only "A Wing and a Prayer."

   S M A R T   P I L L S

➤ Crystallize your goals and objectives before changing your investment options. Analyze existing and optimal levels of employee participation. Evaluate the allocation of your asset base and the pros and cons of various investment fund arrangements.

➤ Formulate your company's position on 404(c) compliance and an education program.

➤ Make plan decisions a team effort. Enlist the help and expertise of your investment group, employee benefits and human resources managers, legal counsel and trustees.

➤ Encourage employee input on plan options, existing and proposed, as well as on communication and education needs.

➤ Know what you are paying for and what each option and service costs. Weigh the cost/benefit ratio of bundled, unbundled and alliance arrangements.

➤ Assess how well your fund choices cover the risk/return spectrum. Is there enough choice for participants at every level of risk tolerance? Strike a balance between ample choice and a manageable, understandable number of options for your employee profile.

➤ Look at fund volatility in various periods as you evaluate the returns of a prospective fund option.

➤ Gather as much intelligence as possible on the merits of different options, products, and services from practitioners, industry associations and providers.

➤ Understand alpha, and let your managers know what you expect them to deliver.

➤ Apply the same rigor to the due diligence process in manager selection as you would for a DB plan.

CHAPTER
TWO

THE BEST OF BOTH WORLDS:
APPLYING DB PRINCIPLES TO YOUR DC PLAN

Nathaniel H. Duffield

*H*alliburton is a global company that provides energy, engineering and construction services through a worldwide workforce of more than 60,000 employees. Six DC plans in the U.S. with more than $3 billion in assets currently cover approximately 45,000 plan participants.

Our first retirement plan grew out of the desire of the company's founder, Erle Halliburton, to share the company's profits with its employees. His tax advisors recommended that the most effective way to accomplish this goal was through a qualified profit sharing plan. As a result, a relatively uncomplicated profit sharing plan was established on January 1, 1944. Were he alive today, Mr. Halliburton would undoubtedly be appalled at how complex that initial plan has become! Nonetheless, the roots of the basic plan still exist, although in substantially changed form.

WHAT MAKES HALLIBURTON'S DC PLAN DIFFERENT?

Halliburton's retirement fund is unique among those of larger companies for many reasons. From the time it was established, defined contribution (DC) programs have remained our primary retirement vehicle. Although most large companies provide DC plans, such plans frequently supplement a primary defined benefit (DB) arrangement. Moreover, unlike Halliburton's, which began a half century ago, DC programs are a relatively recent phenomenon: their real growth only began in the mid-1980's in the form of 401(k) plans.

Perhaps the greatest difference between our plan and others is that at Halliburton we manage our DC programs in the way other companies manage their DB plans. Rather than using mutual funds, we use multiple separate account managers whom we monitor with an internal investment staff. Contrary to present day trends, we prefer an unbundled approach, and we do not outsource recordkeeping or administration.

Our Internal Fund Management Structure

Halliburton's Executive Committee appoints an Investment Committee responsible for establishing the investment policy and objectives for each of our six investment funds. It is also the Investment Committee's responsibility to select external investment managers as well as to monitor these managers and all other trust activities. Our Committee generally meets at least once a quarter; additional meetings are scheduled as necessary.

There are six Committee members: each holds the highest financial management position within our company. As Director, Trust Investments, I chair the Committee. Halliburton's management believes the Committee's decision-making process should be financially driven and that members can best add value when they have a financial background. We are unusual among DC plans in this respect, since the teams overseeing most DC plans are drawn from Human Resources. Because the actual investment decisions are made only by those with financial backgrounds, the Investment Committee can address complex investment issues and make decisions rapidly.

At the same time, however, the Committee realizes that retirement funds cannot be managed in a vacuum, and that regular interaction with Human Resources and plan administration personnel is essential. Thus, plan administrators are invited to attend all Investment Committee meetings. Similarly, I or my associate attends all plan administrative committee meetings as a guest or committee member. This cross attendance creates the kind of teamwork necessary to manage efficiently both the investment funds and plan administration. Ours is a top-down orientation, where decisions made for plan administration purposes do not generally drive the investment management policy.

The day-to-day management of all trust activities is assigned to the Trust Investment Department, which is responsible for both our U.S.-based and worldwide trust investment activities. Our department operates as a part of our Corporate Office since its responsibilities span the entire corporate organization.

Our Trust Investment Department consists of four employees and we have no plans to expand. Working with me are a master trust administrator, a trust accountant and a secretary. One hundred percent of our time is devoted to managing four trust pools in the U.S. and four major international pools. We oversee 24 external investment managers throughout the U.S. and four foreign countries, who together manage 31 different portfolios and assets totaling over U.S. $3.5 billion.

Unlike many other companies, Halliburton's Trust Investment Department *is not part of the company's treasury operation*. It is a stand-alone department that reports directly to the Chief Financial Officer. Senior management believes this separation is desirable due to the completely different investment philosophies used to manage corporate cash and the retirement funds. This separation also indicates the importance management places on the investment management of the retirement funds. Our department is highly visible to top management and accountability is clear.

Consider this:

As you study opportunities, you glide with ease

[for analysts, portfolio managers and traders]

between fundamental research, technical analysis, quotes, news, even real-time

trading—all on one screen. In fact, you've simplified the process even more

[the only fully integrated research and analytics service]

by organizing the information flow to fit your strategy. Click and up pops a list

[fully customizable indicators, signals and screens]

of stocks. A few clicks more and you've filtered the list through sets of fundamental

[access up to 10,000 issues]

and technical parameters that you've defined, quickly paring it to a few select

[screen, sort and rank lists using any combination of data]

candidates. Then you drag and drop these remaining symbols into the charting

window; instantly, you see buy/sell signals and price and volume trends ranging

[customize charts using available indicators or your own]

from intra-day to 13 years. A call for additional expertise is always available. You

[work with a pro-active research and analytics desk]

snap into the trading window, determine activity in each stock and set your

[trade through Instinet in real-time]

strategies. You're closing the gap between information and execution.

You're working with Instinet.

[for information call 800-225-5008]

INSTINET.
A REUTER COMPANY

This is research.

INVESTMENT MANAGEMENT: PHILOSOPHY AND PROCESS

Since our internal staff is small, we only focus on what we feel are the most important parts of the investment management process. We do not micro-manage our funds and we remain unconvinced that more staff would measurably add value.

Some plan sponsors prefer to create paper portfolios with investment managers or build so-called "farm teams" where small amounts of money are given to managers. These "farm team" managers are then monitored over periods of time and, at some point, may be more substantially funded. While this process may acquaint a plan sponsor with a manager's style, we question how much real insight is gained through such a "trial run." We don't believe that short-term performance is a predictable or accurate indicator of future performance.

In contrast, we add an investment manager only after we exercise extensive due diligence. We firmly believe that we can know a manager's organization and investment process far more thoroughly and accurately in a much shorter time frame than we could using the "farm team" approach. Our consultant, SEI Capital Resources, sorts through prospective managers using the information and data accumulated by their manager search specialists. We combine this information with the knowledge we have gathered from our on-site visits to various firms.

After narrowing down the number of managers to those few who appear to best meet our requirements, we again visit each of these organizations. Afterward, one to three managers will be invited to make a formal presentation to our investment committee before our final selection. In most cases, we hold more than just one meeting with managers prior to selection; often these meetings will continue until we are satisfied that one manager meets our requirements. Our ongoing contact with the investment management community facilitates this process.

HOW WE CHOOSE A NEW INVESTMENT MANAGER

Among the criteria we consider important in evaluating a prospective investment manager are:

➤ Fee structure

➤ Organizational structure: Is it adequate to support the type of investment management services we need?

➤ Consistency of past performance

➤ Loss of key personnel: If the CIO, the Head of Research, or our portfolio manager leaves, would that departure have significant impact on fund management and performance?

➤ Compensation arrangements: Are they competitive enough to retain key personnel?

➤ Investment process: Is it compatible with our goals?

➤ Adherence to their management style: Do they have proven consistency?

➤ Ability to manage within our guidelines: Are they responsive to our needs?

- Willingness to work as a member of our team: Do they accept this important aspect of our management philosophy?
- Other investment management capabilities which may be useful to us in the future: Does a domestic manager, for example, also have an international management capability?
- The assignment of portfolio managers: Will there be a good fit?
- Accounts lost: What were the causes? Do they suggest a repetitive pattern? Do they reveal some inherent weakness we should identify?

In the final analysis, *the key factor is how well the manager will blend into our current investment manager group.*

After we have chosen a firm, we fund it sufficiently to make a difference in the overall performance of our investment fund, from both return and risk standpoints. These amounts range from a minimum of 3% of total assets for a highly specialized assignment to a maximum of 10% for a core assignment. We work closely with the manager in the future and attempt to develop a lasting and productive relationship.

How We Support the Investment Manager Team

We also believe in giving our managers enough time — generally three years — to let their discipline succeed. Actually, a market cycle is usually necessary to observe the manager's discipline during both good and bad markets. Experience has taught us that no manager style will always be in favor, and performance often moves in cycles. Patience is a great virtue in investment management, and it is ultimately rewarded over the long term. I will concede that it may be easier for us to be patient than it is for some other plan sponsors; multiple specialty managers don't often perform in tandem through the same market cycles.

Our longer-term view serves another valuable function: it relieves pressure on our investment managers for short-term performance. Not only does this strengthen our long-term relationship with managers, it gives us very low manager turnover, another of our important goals. Relationships with two of our managers, for example, date back to the mid-1970's.

We have terminated manager relationships only six times in the past ten years. Turnover is expensive and disrupts our optimal goal of a seamless investment management strategy. It also tends to destroy the consistency we think extremely important to generate superior long-term investment returns.

But it is important to recognize when a manager relationship should be terminated. *Unsatisfactory performance has rarely been our reason for ending a relationship.* Instead, the trigger has most often been changes in the investment management organization, or a change in our own strategy which renders a given manager's discipline irrelevant or undesirable.

How Do We Exercise Due Diligence?

Due diligence has become an increasingly important part of our internal management focus. We personally meet with each of our managers several times each

Put your nose on Kansas.

Now you see the U.S. the way most domestic asset managers do.

A little too closely.

In today's global economy, domestic portfolios of all countries are heavily influenced by international markets and events. A purely domestic approach to managing these portfolios is as obsolete as the passbook savings account.

Whether you're investing domestically or internationally, what you need is a whole-world perspective.

With regional specialists in all major markets, Barings gives you a more complete and accurate view of investment opportunities anywhere.

A view you'll find nowhere else.

Today, there are no longer "domestic" or "international" managers.

There are simply those who can help you succeed in the world as it is now.

And those who can't.

For more on the unique advantages of Barings' global approach to investment management, call Fraser Blakely at 617-951-0052.

BARINGS

year and at least once at their facilities. These on-site visits are extremely effective and productive. Actually, our ongoing due diligence process differs little from the process we follow during initial hiring; it is just less intense as our familiarity with the manager grows. However, two factors become more important over time: good communication (which is as much our responsibility as the manager's), and the manager's continuing ability to function successfully as a member of Halliburton's team.

Aside from enabling us to meet with key personnel and support people, these on-site visits help foster the in-depth relationships we consider so critical. Because of our belief that it is only possible to deal effectively with a limited number of investment managers, we make every effort to use our managers for multiple purposes. Through our on-site visits we learn what capabilities, beyond portfolio management, our managers have that might help us later in other ways. We currently use six of our investment managers for multiple purposes, an effective cost-control strategy. One of these relationships now crosses international boundaries as they manage a non-U.S. equity portfolio for our U.S. master trust, a portfolio for our U.K. Pooled Pension Plan and an Offshore Bermudan Trust.

WHAT DOES ALL THIS COST?

The 1993 overhead for our Trust Investment Department, paid by the company, amounted to *less than .31% of average net assets*. All expenses required to operate our master trust are charged to the trust, including audit, consulting, investment management and custody. The largest part of this expense is investment management fees which amounted to .29% of average net assets during calendar year 1993. The other expenses charged raised the total operating cost to slightly less than .34%. We generate additional income for the trust through securities lending and commission recapture programs. Together these programs earn 3 basis points, decreasing the net cost of operation to just over .31%.

THE TEAM CONCEPT: A NOT SO "SECRET" TO SUCCESS

The team concept is the foundation of our Trust Investment Department. Each team member fulfills a vital role and we cannot operate efficiently without the effective and expected contributions of each member. It may be somewhat easier to function as a team when you are few in number but even a small group cannot achieve established goals consistently and efficiently if it does not operate as a team.

The same concept is used throughout our investment management structure. Everyone involved in the process is part of the team: our trustee/custodian, investment managers and consultant. Our team member relationships go beyond the limits of the traditional concept of client versus vendor. Effective communication is one key. Everyone knows his or her role in the process and understands the role of every other team member.

At every meeting we ensure that each team member sees the big picture. We examine whether the final goals and objectives are being achieved and, if not, we explore the reasons why. Every team member has to know whether he or she has added or subtracted value and how and why this happened. As an incentive to accomplish team objectives, we lend our support to every team member's organization. Some of these longer-term relationships have evolved into close "strategic alliances."[1]

A PLAN STRUCTURE CUSTOM-DESIGNED FOR HALLIBURTON'S EMPLOYEES

Why six separate plans? Halliburton has three distinct operating groups. Each has its own plan to reflect the characteristics of its particular employee base. Provisions such as profit sharing contribution formulas, vesting scales, the 401(k) company match and distribution methods may vary among plans. The remaining three plans are "frozen" and no longer receive new contributions. In addition, the IRS restricts certain designated protected benefits from being down-graded, and we have therefore had difficulty merging plans. Rather than constantly changing the provisions of our basic plans, we have preferred to maintain these plans separately. Although there are certain differences among our DC plans, the basic transfer and investment option features among the six are identical.

For investment management purposes, the assets of all plans are consolidated into a master trust arrangement. Plan participants have three basic investment options: a Diversified Fund, an Equity Investment Fund and a Fixed Income Fund, with a Company Stock Fund as a fourth, restricted[2] option. Each fund is valued and reconciled monthly. A unitized accounting approach is used for each investment fund, as well as for the individual plans participating in the master trust.

Plan participants may transfer among the four investment options on a monthly basis based upon month-end valuations. They can communicate transfer instructions either via a voice response system or by completing a transfer form. Voice response may also be used to start or change payroll deduction contributions, to receive current account balances and to hear a brief description of investment options.

The active individual plans underlying the master trust are all structured to give participants three ways to accumulate retirement funds: these three features are not stand-alone plans but are combined into one overall plan. All three active DC plans offer all three features:

➤ a company funded profit-sharing feature
➤ an after-tax, payroll deduction savings feature
➤ a 401(k) feature with a company match (the company match formula varies by plan)

I should point out that there is a seventh plan: a DB plan, available only to the participants in our Energy Services group. It is not their primary retirement vehicle, but serves as a back-up benefit to the primary DC plan. We call it a "Floor Plan" since it exists to guarantee a minimum benefit level. It is activated only if the profit-sharing segment of the DC plan fails to provide this minimum benefit.

---

[1] "Strategic alliances" often refer to close working relationships that blur traditional boundaries between client and manager and encourage benefits to both. For example, a manager may provide special research to his plan sponsor client that would not normally be expected; or a sponsor might provide ideas for a new product development to his manager.
[2] See section entitled The Company Funds: Sharing in Halliburton's Future Growth for full explanation of the Company Stock Fund's restrictions.

The "Floor Plan" was created as a result of the 1991 slump in the energy industry, when profit-sharing formula contributions declined and management was concerned that employees might be disadvantaged during downturns. Today, the assets of this "Floor Plan" represent a very minor portion of the total master trust.

"THE DIVERSIFIED FUND": A GLOBAL PIONEER

While we consider all our options diversified, our "Diversified Fund" (internally known as the "General Investment Fund") is highly diversified in several different asset classes. With assets totaling $1.6 billion, it is designed for long-term growth. The investment policy targets 62% for investment in stocks, about 30% in non-U.S. securities. Five percent of the overall stock allocation is invested in emerging markets. Another 8% of our Diversified Fund is targeted for a global bond strategy which makes extensive use of non-U.S. fixed income securities.

Halliburton's Diversified Fund has invested in non-U.S. securities since early 1985. Some observers may think that our early and significant allocation in non-U.S. securities has been quite aggressive for a DC plan, but we see it as a great tool for diversification. In fact, diversification as a risk control technique is fundamental to our investment strategies. As a global company with operations in many emerging markets, our exposure to these markets makes considerable investment sense. Our working knowledge of foreign markets has enabled us to move into this asset class more swiftly than other DC plans.

This fund is further diversified by our use of multiple external investment managers with varying investment styles. Sixteen different managers manage six different asset classes for the Diversified Fund.

Since the Diversified Fund evolved from our original profit sharing plan, almost all active plan participants participate. Additionally, there is approximately $150 million of retired life monies invested here. We believe this fund has been very popular with participants largely because they do not have to make their own asset allocation decisions.

Halliburton has also been quite successful in fulfilling its long-term growth objective for the fund. Over a ten-year period, the Diversified Fund has achieved an annualized return very close to a pure equity return (using the S&P 500 as a benchmark) — with much less risk than the stock market itself. Its annualized rates of return through 1993 are shown below compared to the S&P 500 and the percentile ranking in the Wilshire Trust Universe Comparison System (TUCS) for all master trusts.

	RETURN (Rank)		
	1 Year	5 Years	10 Years
Halliburton Diversified Fund	17.1% (13)	14.0% (15)	14.7% (6)
S&P 500	10.0%	14.5%	14.9%

THE EQUITY INVESTMENT FUND:
LONG-TERM GROWTH WITH LESS RISK

Our newest investment option, the Equity Investment Fund, was created on January 1, 1994 after we realized that the average age of plan participants had

dropped significantly. Since equities have historically produced better investment returns over the long term, we felt that many of our younger plan participants should have an option that would offer equity returns without the same degree of risk as the equity market itself.

Certainly, we worked very diligently over the years to create an equity exposure for the Diversified Fund that was meaningfully diversified through assets and the use of multiple management styles. (We have seven U.S. equity investment managers and four non-U.S. equity managers.) We asked ourselves why we needed an entirely new equity strategy. How feasible would it be to segregate the Diversified Fund's equity exposures to create a new fund? What were the cost ramifications? Which alternative would be in the best interest of plan participants?

As we explored our alternatives, we came rapidly to the conclusion that it would be very easy and cost-effective to segregate the equity pool of the Diversified Fund and use it for dual purposes: it could also serve as a pure equity investment option. The technology existed at State Street Bank, our master trustee and custodian, to sub-unitize this pool from an accounting standpoint, thereby facilitating its use for multiple purposes. From that point on, it was merely an accounting exercise, one that would be transparent to the investment managers who continued to manage just one account and one pool of assets. This structure continues to work very well for us.

The investment objective of the Equity Investment Fund is to achieve long-term growth by investing primarily in stocks and related securities. The longer-term returns of our Diversified Fund have been very good but the equity segment of this fund has done much better. Although the Equity Investment Fund is more aggressively structured, and therefore riskier than the Diversified Fund, we continue to stress risk control. We believe participants are much more likely to invest in equities if volatility is mitigated.

As noted, one way we mitigate risk is to use multiple investment managers. Six of our seven managers are traditional and are matched by their varying styles or approaches to the investment management process. The seventh manager uses an options overwriting strategy, transparent to the other managers, overlaying the entire domestic equity portfolio.

Since 1990, we have used various index options to write out-of-the-money calls, receive the related premium and hope that the market doesn't have a continuing upward spike that calls the options away. We have always known that we would sacrifice some of our equity return in a continually surging stock market. However, since a surging market occurs infrequently, we feel that the strategy increases our equity return incrementally in most other market environments. Most important, this strategy lowers our risk and volatility, and has performed exactly as we expected.

Although the Equity Investment Fund has not existed as a separate fund for a ten-year period, we do have the historical data on the equity segment of the Diversified Fund, its precursor. The annualized rates of return for the equity segment through 1993 are shown below compared to the S&P 500 and the percentile ranking in TUCS for all master trusts.

	RETURN (Rank)[3]		
	1 Year	5 Years	10 Years
Halliburton Equity Investment Fund	14.4% (35)	17.4% (7)	17.8% (1)
S&P 500	10.0%	14.5%	14.9%

THE FIXED INCOME FUND: STABLE RATES OF RETURN

In 1976 Halliburton introduced an after-tax savings feature that enables plan participants to contribute to the plan through payroll deductions. We created the Fixed Income Fund as an option for participants who might not want to risk their own monies in the more aggressively postured Diversified Fund. Besides preservation of principal, the investment objective of the Fixed Income Fund is to generate a reasonable and relatively stable rate of return.

Within six years the asset base of this fund reached about $50 million. Beginning in 1983, the Fixed Income Fund experienced explosive growth, helped along by the introduction of the 401(k) feature. Today, the Fund's assets are approaching $1.4 billion, and its growth requires considerable investment attention.

For a fund of its type, we believe that the Fixed Income Fund is highly diversified. About 45% is invested in traditional fixed income assets and cash equivalents managed by six external investment managers. Although these portfolios use different strategies, they are all fairly conservative. Most have limited-duration horizons and are relatively high-quality portfolios. Conservative as this segment of the fund might be, it is still subject to interim volatility as the general interest rate environment changes. We balance this segment of the Fund with what we refer to as the "book value" portion (named for the accounting concept applied to GICs) which represents the other 55% of the fund.

---

[3] SEI Capital Resources recently completed a study which indicates that the Equity Investment Fund would be more efficient from a risk and return standpoint if the non-U.S. equities were included. We plan to include the non-U.S. segment by mid-year 1994.

Until seven years ago our Fixed Income Fund was 100% invested in traditional GICs. Then, because of declining credit quality in the life insurance industry, we felt it was prudent to diversify into other types of investments. Due to the lack of alternatives at the time, we turned to actively managed bond portfolios. Since then, we have yet to invest any funds in a traditional GIC. Our search for alternatives to traditional GICs led to our early use of asset-backed separate accounts ("wrapped portfolios") and synthetic GIC contracts.

We were among the first to invest in these two pioneering products developed by Metropolitan Life Insurance Company and Bankers Trust. Both separate accounts and synthetic GICs utilize an actively managed portfolio underlying a book value contract. Today 23% of our Fixed Income Fund, about $340 million, is invested in these asset-backed contracts.

We are quite pleased with the results and it is very likely that we will use more in the future. The business is expanding rapidly as more financial institutions and investment managers develop new products. I believe this is a very healthy trend since competition will make these contracts more cost-effective and new products will continue to offer more innovative ways to diversify.

A word of warning: synthetic GIC instruments are generally very complex and are not for the unsophisticated. Plan sponsors interested in these vehicles would do well to get expert advice before investing.

The annualized returns of the Fixed Income Fund are shown below for periods of one, five, and seven years through year-end 1993.

Years:	One	Five	Seven
Fixed Income Fund	8.0%	9.5%	9.9%

THE COMPANY FUND: SHARING IN HALLIBURTON'S FUTURE GROWTH

Introduced in mid-1987, the Company Stock Fund today has assets of approximately $73 million. Its sole investment fund is Halliburton Company common stock, and its purpose is to give employees the opportunity to participate in the company's future growth. Recognizing that our DC plans are our participants' primary retirement vehicle, and that investment risk is borne directly by the plan participants, management decided to de-emphasize this fund and, in fact, restrict participant investment in it. Participant contributions cannot be invested; only company contributed monies can be transferred into the fund. Even then, we limit it to only 15% of each participant's company contribution accounts.

THE IMPORTANCE OF CUSTODY

In 1986 we began to question the effectiveness of managing separately the assets of the company's six different DC plans. Although the plans were different, their basic structures were the same. We thought that substantial efficiency could be gained by pooling the assets for investment management purposes: we could realize cost advantages, similar investment returns, and more importantly, consistent diversification.

The master trust concept, although well established by that time, was not widely

Defined by our commitment

to a disciplined, proven investment

process

Investing with Chancellor means
investing in a process—a clearly
defined, repeatable, rigorous
approach to asset management.
Our process is characterized by a
disciplined interplay of fundamental
and quantitative resources, developed and refined by the same group
of investment professionals who
have been working together, in many
cases, for more than a decade.

The positive results of Chancellor's process are realized by our clients year after year: superior returns, controlled risk, and stable lasting relationships that genuinely contribute toward the fulfillment of client objectives.

Distinguished by our

superior long-term

results

 Chancellor Capital Management

used by DC plans. Yet, it seemed to be the perfect vehicle for our consolidation efforts. At the beginning of 1987, we became one of the first plan sponsors to commingle all DC assets in one master trust. This is still an uncommon practice, and it is particularly rare to see a combination of consolidated assets and active management. The success of this structure has far exceeded our expectations. Management has been extremely pleased with the consolidated reporting capabilities and greater investment control, both advantageous to our global operation.

This process has worked so well for us in the U.S. that, subsequently, we used a similar approach for three foreign retirement plan asset pools. Interestingly, asset consolidation prompted us to review and, where feasible, to begin to combine our various DC plans. Consolidation has vastly simplified plan administration. A top-down approach of dealing with the assets first has improved the efficiency of the underlying plan administration.

We applied the same rationale to our search for a global custodian for our foreign pension plans, which were growing rapidly. State Street Bank and Trust Company has enabled us to cope with a very complex management structure while we keep our own staff very small. We continue to manage the process rather than manage the people.

INVESTMENT OPTIONS: HOW MANY ARE JUST RIGHT?

Our four investment options clearly indicate our reluctance to add a myriad of options. One reason may be our experience in building our DC program layer by layer. A second and crucial reason is that our DC plan is our primary retirement program.

We have concentrated on a few basic options that can produce the growth needed for a capital accumulation program without any more risk than necessary. We have managed these options intensely.

In addition, our operational management has resisted increasing the number of investment options because our participants are scattered around the world, creating an enormous communications challenge. These managers have also questioned the wisdom of forcing a participant to make complex asset allocation decisions that will, undoubtedly, have a critical effect on his or her final retirement benefit. This rationale is particularly compelling when the participant is working in the wastelands of Russia or in the far corners of China. Although some cynical observers may call us "paternalistic," we always consider what is in the best interest of our plan participants.

There is probably no one answer to the question of how many options are enough or, for that matter, how many are too many. Demographics differ among companies and retirement programs vary. A retirement program that has a supplemental DC plan may have different objectives than one like ours. The Department of Labor's 404(c) rule may establish a minimum number of options for plans electing to comply, but it still clearly considers plan fiduciaries responsible for prudently managing the options, regardless of the number.

INVESTMENT OPTIONS: WHY NOT MUTUAL FUNDS?

How to construct the best combination of investment options also depends on many elements, including the size of the plan assets, the company's demographics and what the plan sponsor thinks is prudent. Halliburton stands by its highly diversified, intensely managed approach.

Why not use mutual funds? Popular with many 401(k) plans, mutual funds are a reasonable choice for plans with smaller asset bases that, nonetheless, need to achieve some diversification. But it would be difficult, for instance, to apply our version of the due diligence process to the typical mutual fund organization.

How often could a plan sponsor walk into a mutual fund's headquarters, for instance, and meet personally with the portfolio manager, the research staff and support team? Could a plan sponsor reasonably expect to influence a mutual fund's investment guidelines and restrictions?

Moreover, what impact can the plan sponsor have on controlling the costs of a mutual fund operation? Is the mutual fund making good use of the assets under its control by using a well conceived securities lending program? How efficient is it at controlling trading costs? Is it using "soft dollars?" These questions can be answered easily by any investment management firm, but answers are less accessible from mutual fund companies.

As a case in point, our net operating costs in 1993 amounted to about .31% of average net assets. The Morningstar Mutual Fund Report gives the 1993 average expense ratio for all mutual funds as 1.11%. Certainly, our lower expense ratio can be attributed partly to our large asset base, but our investment management structure is also much more complex and customized than most single mutual funds which ought to make our costs that much greater.

Finally, most mutual funds operate with only one management style. It is therefore difficult to achieve the in-depth diversification that varying investment management styles and disciplines offer. The blending of styles can only be achieved through multiple mutual funds chosen by plan participants.

CROSS-MANAGEMENT: A TREND FOR THE FUTURE

Many plan sponsors, particularly those with larger DB plans, put as much or more effort than we do into managing their DB asset base. They have investment management relationships that could easily be transferred to their DC programs. Doing this would appear to be quite cost-effective, as well, since the due diligence process is already in place and little extra effort would be required. In fact, I have recently seen several plan sponsors begin to make use of their DB investment management relationships to manage their DC plan. This makes a great deal of sense and is very likely in the best interest of plan participants. I think we are likely to see more of this type of cross-management in the future.

PLAN ADMINISTRATION

At Halliburton, Human Resources oversees our plan administration although, as discussed, our Trust Investment Department interfaces regularly with this department.

All of our DC plan administration is handled internally. The voice response system has been in place since 1991 and it is probably the single most effective change we have made to our plan administration in years. Most notably, this system has eliminated the need to issue quarterly account balance statements since participants can call in at any time for this information. All we need issue is an annual statement of account.

Since its installation, the use of voice response has steadily increased: the system currently handles about 7,000 calls each month. Roughly 16% of Halliburton's 45,000 active participants make one call per month.[4] To ensure confidentiality, each participant must encode his or her own Personal Identification Number before accessing account information.

RECORDKEEPING: AN INTERNAL FUNCTION

Participant recordkeeping is, as it has always been, an internal function. After conducting a complete review of our old system in 1986, we decided to build a new recordkeeping administration system.

After exploring external alternatives, it was clear none could as effectively automate our many complex requirements as we could ourselves. We designed, constructed and installed a new system in late 1987.

Our in-house system continues to serve us well. It was designed to be flexible, to anticipate and successfully meet a variety of inevitable future changes. The recordkeeping program is a real-time, on-line system capable of handling multiple investment options and DC plans, while it integrates the requirements of our DB Floor Plan. It also has flexible reporting capabilities. Our Information Services Center is responsible for the system's daily operation.

This same recordkeeping system also supports our Canadian DC plan, interfaces with our several payroll systems, and integrates an extensive retiree distribution system. Any company location can access the system. Recently, after reviewing our system, one of the nation's major providers of participant recordkeeping services recommended that we continue to use our own internal system.

HOW WE OFFER SERVICE TO OUR RETIREES

Perhaps it seems strange that a retiree distribution system is integrated with the recordkeeping systems. Yet all our DC plans offer three basic distribution options to our retirees: payment in a lump sum, a purchased annuity, or payment in monthly installments drawn against the account balance while the remaining balance continues to earn returns. The monthly installment option has become the preferred method and we issue over 4,000 distributions to retirees each month.

This system is fully automated, allowing for electronic deposit and deduction for such things as taxes and insurance premiums. Retirees with account balances are offered the same investment options and the same monthly transfer features as the active participants. In fact, the reason that our Fixed Income Fund has assets of almost $1.4 billion is not that our participants are overly conservative investors, *but that over 50% of the assets belong to retired life account balances.* This feature may be unique among all DC plans.[5]

---

[4] Actually, use is probably higher since these numbers reflect 800 usage and participants based overseas cannot access the 800 number.

[5] Halliburton recognizes its educational responsibilities to its retirees as well as to its current employees and, from time to time, in addition to regular information mailings, holds seminars specifically for retirees to brief them on current developments in their investment options and plan participation.

Outsourcing Recordkeeping: A Cost Advantage?

Increasingly, DC plans are outsourcing recordkeeping to reduce costs. From time to time we, too, have explored the possibility of outsourcing and we will probably look again in the future. However, we have yet to discover a significant cost advantage because of the unique complexity of our plan structure.

But in our view, control is as important as cost. Certainly, anyone choosing to maintain their recordkeeping internally must ensure that the responsibility will receive greater internal company priority than operational functions, as it does at Halliburton. We believe that administrative control and direct participant contact are maintained with an internal system, which are two major advantages. If things are not working well with an internal arrangement, it only takes a corporate decision to correct matters. On the other hand, a forced change in external recordkeepers can be expensive and disruptive.

To Bundle or Unbundle?

One heated DC plan debate today centers on whether a bundled or unbundled approach is best: that is, whether to obtain all investment management, participant recordkeeping and some aspects of plan administration services through one provider or many. It is clear that Halliburton is not a proponent of the bundled approach. Our preferences may again be driven somewhat by the complexities of our retirement program, but in large part they reflect insights we have gained through the half century evolution of our DC system.

My greatest concern about a bundled approach is the due diligence process. If the due diligence effort reveals a problem with a single part of a bundled program, can it be corrected easily? Probably not. Since all services are tied together, it may be impossible to disengage the parts. How many times will a plan sponsor be willing to move the entire bundle to a new provider? Who will pay for any losses incurred by such a problem? The real costs of a DC program can be measured in many ways, including lost opportunity. This brings us to the central fiduciary question again: are the decisions being made in the best interests of the company — or of the plan participants?

Transfer Options: Quarterly, Monthly or Daily?

In 1993 we switched from a quarterly to a monthly transfer option. The move was easy since we were already valuing and reconciling each investment fund monthly. The choice of a quarterly, monthly or daily transfer option really depends upon one's view of the real purpose of the transfer capability and the advantages of a speedy transfer. A quarterly transfer feature may soon become standard since compliance with 404(c) requires at least a quarterly option. Although the daily option has grown increasingly popular; we are opposed to it for many reasons.

The transfer feature, like any investment option the plan offers, should enable the participant to alter easily his or her investment structure to adjust to changing personal financial requirements. Yet, retirement financial goals are for most people relatively long-term in nature.

Our fundamental belief is that investing should be approached with a longer-term view. The movement of financial markets over a period of one day, one

"Risk Arbitrage, Bankruptcy and Distressed Real Estate can be your least volatile investments in a prudently managed portfolio."

John M. Angelo, CEO
Angelo, Gordon & Co.

Risk Arbitrage, Bankruptcy

Angelo, Gordon defines risk arbitrage as "…situations with a begining, a middle and an analyzable conclusion." These are mostly short term investments in announced tenders and mergers.

Bankruptcy investment is considered in the same light but the conclusion can take from one to three years. Combining Risk Arbitrage and Bankruptcy results in portfolios of staggered maturities offering a predictable income stream.

Distressed Real Estate

Angelo, Gordon also specializes in distressed real estate assets, purchasing sub-performing and non-performing mortgages and properties. By prudent management of the underlying assets we are able to generate current yields of over 10% and expect all-in returns of over 20%. We focus on $5 to $20 million transactions—too big for most local real estate investors and too small for large capital pools.

Angelo, Gordon & Co.

Our portfolios are always diversified and typically unleveraged. Since our formation in 1988, we have continued to invest for our clients under a strict investment philosophy generating superior returns with low volatility.

If this thinking appeals to you, call John Angelo at **(212) 692-2020**.

Assets Under Management
(In Millions)

Angelo, Gordon & Co. Experts in investments insulated from market fluctuation.

month, or even one year, can be the result of short-term noise and lack any real meaning. We consider market-timing a loser's game — in many years in the investment industry I have seen few who have been consistently successful with this approach. Introducing a daily transfer feature to permit market-timing seems to me to be somewhat dangerous.

Does daily valuation actually encourage participants to market-time or to react, after the fact, to major short-term market changes? Quite possibly. Apart from the issue of whether daily valuation actually benefits the participant, is its expense to the company or plan sponsor. And in reality, a complete daily reconciliation is very difficult, if not impossible. Who will absorb the costs if substantial errors occur, the company or the plan participant?

COMMUNICATION, EDUCATION OR ADVICE?

The biggest risk of all for plan participants is failing to accumulate an adequate retirement benefit. Obviously, part of the accumulation in a DC plan derives from contributions by both the participant and the company. But *how* participants invest their monies is the critical component. To help participants achieve their retirement objectives, plan sponsors must implement and maintain a substantive communication/ education program that compensates for the increased investment management responsibility they bear.

Communication is one of the most pressing issues confronting plan sponsors today. Faced with numerous investment options and lacking investment sophistication and skills, many participants simply cannot make informed choices. The educational needs of most participants demand an increasingly large share of plan resources. Most plan sponsors are not organized or staffed to run a continuous and consistent program and the question of what constitutes legal advice remains unclear.

There are many creative and useful approaches for communication/education programs including focus groups, regular newsletters, various forms of printed material and specialized software for the personal computer.

HALLIBURTON'S COMMUNICATION/EDUCATION PROGRAM

Our own approach has been fragmented and we realize the urgency and need to improve our communication/education program. We are currently exploring several alternatives; most of them will stress participant education in investment matters as well as in retirement planning.

The most consistent part of our current communication/education effort has been an annual report on the financial aspects of our investment funds. This report, launched in the mid-1980's, provides some investment education in addition to detailed information on the financial status of the various investment funds. It is distributed to the plan participants along with their annual statement of account. Although we have steadily improved this report over the years, it is not sufficient.

We have used focus groups intermittently to get direct input from plan participants as well as to disseminate information regarding our investment options. Participant input was somewhat successful, but these groups proved to be disappointing as a means of distributing information.

One of our operating groups produces its own quarterly benefits-related newsletter. I often contribute articles on specific investment topics which invariably elicit a positive response, according to that unit's benefits manager. Though I consider this effort in itself insufficient and too after-the-fact, it seems to be a valuable tool that I endorse using on a company-wide basis.

Halliburton is currently exploring the possibility of a quarterly communication focused on pre-retirement planning as well as on investment related issues. This letter, distributed throughout the company, can be a useful supplement to the information in our annual financial report.

Our Human Resources Department may conduct a benefits survey among participants which would include questions about effective communication/education methods. We have also reviewed the efforts of many other plan sponsors who are leaders in DC plan communication and are considering recommendations from some of our investment managers.

THE PROBLEM OF COMMUNICATIONS DISTRIBUTION

For large companies, distributing plan communications and education materials is a considerable challenge. Unfortunately, due to Halliburton's corporate organization, I have no control over anything other than investment communications. Beyond the annual report, we have no means of regularly distributing communications from the corporate level. Furthermore, the cost of communications is an operating unit expense. Even if it were not, only the individual operating units could guarantee that each of their participants would receive materials, since each has its own personnel and payroll system, for example.

Mundane as it may seem, distribution costs can be a big deterrent to expanding the communication and education effort for many companies. Postage costs alone for many mailings, including all the fund prospectuses required by 404(c), can be substantial, especially when you include all the retirees who, as in our case, are still actively invested. Mounting a coordinated, ongoing communications and education effort poses a big challenge for the plan sponsor.

A FINAL THOUGHT

The rapid movement away from DB to DC plans has spawned some trendy new services and arrangements. You have concluded by now, no doubt, that Halliburton has never been a trend follower. But we are consistently open to new ideas, and I always find it helpful to hear how others approach a similar problem or objective. The world of DC plans today is a complex and sometimes treacherous one. Help is always welcome.

➤ Establish clear, understandable and obtainable objectives. Investment policy objectives should specifically quantify risk tolerance as well as long-term investment return benchmarks.

➤ Recognize the strength of a team effort where everyone is committed to clearly articulated goals and objectives.

➤ Define clearly the roles and responsibilities of every member of the team.

➤ Maintain an intense and continuous due diligence effort. Formulate your definition of prudence and establish procedures to achieve and document it.

➤ Build strong, long-term relationships with outside managers.

➤ Maintain an effective cost management program. Consistently review current costs, evaluate their necessity and develop methods to lower and control them.

➤ Change managers when goals are no longer compatible or performance is disappointing over a reasonable period of time.

➤ Establish a structure that gives participants some flexibility — but not too much. Too many options may confuse plan participants and cause more harm than good.

➤ Current trends may, or may not, be what is best for your plan. Will a new trend really benefit your plan or does it seem attractive because everyone else seems to find it so?

➤ Focus on long-term growth.

➤ Establish and develop an effective, ongoing and consistent communication and education program. Review the ways other plan sponsors are approaching this challenge and explore how your current vendors can help.

TRUTH OR CONSEQUENCES IN DC PLAN MANAGEMENT

Sally Gottlieb

Defined Contribution (DC) plans have experienced explosive growth in recent years, and for good reason. They are popular with employees and can be adapted to fit a wide range of company objectives and funding levels. But their popularity has created problems for plan sponsors, particularly in how we position the plans and present and explain them to employees. As the benefits manager for Apple Computer, Inc., a Fortune 100 company with more than 8,000 U.S. employees, I am intimately aware of both the day-to-day and the long-term challenges of creating and sustaining effective, successful DC plans.

Recently a woman about fifty who had worked for Apple for a little more than five years struck up a conversation with me in the cafeteria. "I love the 401(k) plan!" she said. "I've already saved $50,000 in it — more than I was able to save in my whole life!" My immediate reaction was conflict. As Apple's benefits manager and the plan sponsor, I wanted to say, "That's great! Isn't the plan wonderful?" But another part of me wanted to add, "Don't you realize that at that rate you'll never have enough to retire on comfortably at a reasonable age?"

This incident epitomizes the dilemma that many DC plan sponsors face. Although we know the mixed message must be clarified, we have focused almost exclusively on communicating only the positive aspects of the retirement plan. Our intentions are good: we want employees to appreciate the plan and, by extension, the company that provides it. Some of us have trouble getting employees to participate; we have the added objective of getting them involved. As a result, employees may be expecting more from the plan that it can provide. How can we mix in a little reality — making employees aware of the limitations of the plan — without weakening their positive perceptions of it? Before we can answer that question, we need to understand how we got where we are. A quick look back at the trends that triggered the rapid rise of DC plans will help explain.

HOW DID WE GET HERE?

Twenty years ago, the mainstay of most large company benefit programs was the retirement plan, typically a traditional Defined Benefit (DB) plan. By the mid-70's, most such plans became noncontributory; in other words, employees became automatically eligible for the benefit. Employees had no choices to make: the plan was simply there, a benefit built up over time. One day, at retirement, there was a pension.

There have always been certain frustrations for plan sponsors inherent in DB plans: they represent one of the biggest cost items in the benefits package and employees have understood and appreciated them the least.[1] And for younger employees especially, the pay-off seems far off and the formulas complicated and hard to apply to individual circumstances.

The situation hasn't been helped much by the typical plan communications which report in an annual benefit statement to employees the value of their accrued benefit. Since these plans reward long service, and typically pay out most at the point of retirement, the accrued value for younger, shorter-service employees looks pretty paltry.

Another important drawback with DB plans is their lack of portability. For employees, this means that if they leave a company before they are vested, the pension benefit may be lost altogether or, even if they are vested it will, at best, freeze in value until it can be paid out.

With the advent of 401(k) legislation in 1978 and ensuing IRS regulations in 1981,[2] companies began to add a 401(k) plan to the benefits package. Typically, these plans gave employees the option to contribute. If they elected to do so, some of their contributions would be matched by the company. These plans were communicated through a quarterly statement, not unlike a bank statement, which showed the contributions and earnings accruing.

In contrast to DB plans, employees found DC plans easier to understand, as reflected in Hewitt survey results. More frequent reports detailing the buildup of assets gave employees the sense that the plan was a valuable and growing benefit. A younger employee could relate to it more easily because the balances could quickly become larger than those in a personal bank account. An older employee beginning to think about retirement could see its value from that perspective, as well.

The appeal of DC plans comes from their personal nature. For the vast numbers of Baby Boomers, who tend to mistrust institutions (especially the solvency of Social Security) and want to control their own destiny, the appeal of DC plans is obvious. Each employee has his or her own account, and can choose how much to contribute and what funds to invest in. The DC plan account balance "belongs" to the employee, who sees the buildup of value as a result of his or her own actions, judgment and choices. With a growing sense of ownership comes a greater sense of involvement and appreciation. And as the upheaval of frequent job-changing continues in the corporate world, the portability of DC plans means they meet the needs of today's employees far more effectively than DB plans can.

Ongoing improvements in administrative functions have brought employees such conveniences as daily valuation. Employees can get daily fund closing values, move

---

[1] Data extract from Hewitt's Perception Index Database representative of 35 companies with 250,000 employees as of May 1994. Hewitt Associates, Lincolnshire, Illinois.

[2] The Revenue Act of 1978 added Section 401(k) to the Internal Revenue Code, effective January 1, 1980. Proposed regulations issued in November, 1981 sanctioned the use of salary reduction as a source of plan contributions.

money among investment funds easily, and redirect their future investment allocations quickly. Even if most employees don't take advantage of these features, their perception of the plan's flexibility to meet their changing needs improves dramatically.

There are many advantages in DC plans, especially for small companies. They can establish a 401(k) plan at low cost with no initial company matching contributions. As the company grows, it can add a company match based on profits; in a profitable period, when the company can afford it, the contributions can be larger. This added benefit connects employees more directly to the company's business results and provides a strong incentive for high performance.

Apple provides a typical example of this evolution. The company began in 1976 as a small startup with one product, the personal computer. The initial compensation package included basic medical benefits and a competitive pay package that was highly leveraged through bonus programs, cash profit sharing, and stock options. There were no long-term benefits. By 1986, the personal computer industry had taken off: the company was at $1.6 billion in revenues with 4,500 employees and beginning the start of a steep growth curve. To enhance recruiting and retention, the benefits program was expanded to include flexible benefits with a range of medical plan, dental and life insurance options, plus a sabbatical program. At this time, Apple also introduced a 401(k) plan, with employee contributions only.

In 1987 and 1988, Apple doubled its revenues twice and grew to 9000 employees. In 1988, again to enhance the industry-wide competitive standing of the plan, a company match was added to the 401(k) plan. The match was based on service, starting at 30 cents on the dollar and stopping at 50 cents with five years of service. By 1989 participation in the plan ran close to 75%.

In 1990, we took a closer look at the recordkeeping and investment alternatives of the plan. The plan funds were valued quarterly, an intense administrative effort from a staff of six. The quarterly reconciliation process was so laborious it took ten weeks. Quarterly statements were held up until the process was complete. For employees, the process was just as cumbersome: paper forms were required for every transaction, transactions were slow to be processed and results were even slower getting back to employees.

By putting both the recordkeeping and fund management out to bid, we were able to convert the plan to daily valuation and give employees access to daily fund values via telephone. Some plan transactions, such as exchanging money among the investment funds and redirecting future contributions, can also be done over the phone. Best of all, quarterly statements were issued within ten days of the end of the quarter. A year after the conversion was completed, the staff needed to run the plan was reduced to three and service to employees had improved measurably.

Apple has not been unique in improving its 401(k) plan, either in the benefits provided or in its service and administration. According to a 1993 survey of high technology companies,[3] 100% of companies with 200 or more employees offer DC plans, but only 16% of them offer DB plans. The most common changes from the previous year were adding or changing investment options, changing administration or recordkeeper, and adding or increasing the company matching contributions.

These trends have resulted in an explosive growth in the number of DC plans, in some cases at the expense of DB plans, many of which have been terminated. In fact, a recent survey of more than 1500 enrolled actuaries[4] found that more than 30,000 U.S. employers have terminated DB plans since 1990, and of them, nearly 40% have not provided a replacement pension plan. Today, a growing number of companies offers DC plans as their sole retirement plan. But the problem doesn't end there: even companies that provide both DB and DC plans may not realize that the DB plan cannot fulfill its intended purpose for employees who change companies, an occurrence more and more common today.

WHAT DOES ALL THIS MEAN?

Eventually, many employees will need to rely on retirement income from their DC plan, Social Security payments and any personal savings. This is the reality that brings us to critical questions for DC plan sponsors:

> ➤ Will these sources yield enough income for employees to retire on comfortably or adequately?

> ➤ If they don't, why should company plan sponsors care?

> ➤ If we should care, or do care, what should we be doing about it now?

WILL THERE BE ENOUGH FOR RETIREMENT?

Conventional wisdom says that an individual will need 60 to 80% of final income replaced at retirement to maintain the same standard of living enjoyed during his or her working years, assuming a 3% inflation rate. In my opinion, however, conventional wisdom needs to be reevaluated.

---

[3] Radford Associates Benefits Exchange for the High-Tech Industries, San Jose, California, 1993, pp. D1-D4. A 1992 survey of 684 employers from the Wyatt COMPARE Database who represented 7.9 million employees (Wyatt Company, Washington, D.C., 1992), showed the most common trends included adding investment funds, increasing plan valuation frequency, maximum employee contribution and company match.

[4] Survey by the American Academy of Pension Actuaries, Arlington, Va., 1993, p.1.

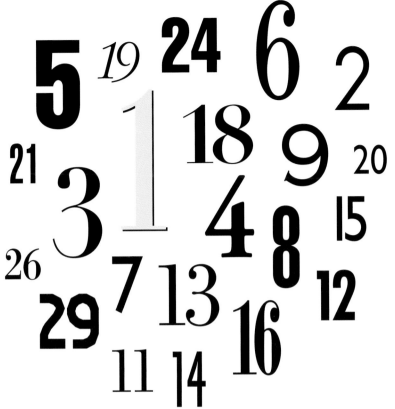

There's 1 in every crowd.

The world is full of also-rans. But in every category there's always a leader. Just one.

In retirement services, that title is held by Fidelity. But we didn't give ourselves that title. You did. The fact is, more companies trust Fidelity for their defined contribution plan needs than any other — half the Fortune 500 alone.

It isn't hard to see why. Fidelity takes the extra measures that keep you out in front. Not only in investment practices, but in technology, service, and innovation. Take a long look at your own plan needs. Ask yourself if your participants deserve the services of a leader, or of a follower.

Then call Fidelity.

Fidelity Institutional Retirement Services Company
82 Devonshire Street, ZZ6, Boston, MA 02109
1-800-343-9184

A DIVISION OF FIDELITY INVESTMENTS INSTITUTIONAL SERVICES
COMPANY (NASD MEMBER) FIDELITY DISTRIBUTORS CORPORATION

51594

➤ Present life expectancies are 20 to 30 years past retirement, so inflation will erode pension and retirement savings unless employees start with more savings and continue to save into retirement.

➤ With increasing workforce mobility, it's not uncommon for employees to move several times during their career which often means starting over on a 30-year mortgage fairly late in the game. It's less likely, therefore, that their house will be paid off around age 65.

➤ Finally, the availability of medical care in retirement is uncertain. This can be a source of huge expense to a retiree if it is only partially covered by the company's retiree medical plan.

Several of the major consulting companies have developed models of retirement needs that present the situation very clearly. For example, Towers Perrin's Strategic Retirement Planning model shows graphically the income needs of retirees, using a company's specific demographics. **Chart 1** compares expenses to income from various sources for an employee earning $50,000 per year before retirement.[5] *The model illustrates the shortfall that employees will experience, unless the company provides or enhances its retirement plans or the employees save money on their own.*

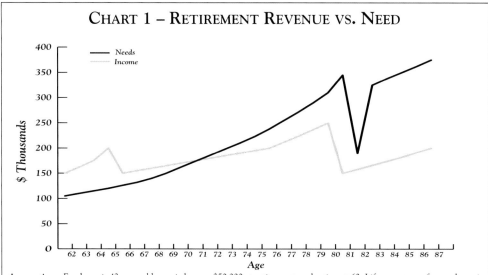

CHART 1 – RETIREMENT REVENUE VS. NEED

Assumptions: Employee is 42 years old, married, earns $50,000 at retirement, and retires at 62. Life expectancy for employee is 81; for spouse is 86. Spouse will enter Long Term Care facility at age 83. Other assumptions on salary increases, inflation, and benefits have been made. Income comes from Social Security, defined benefit and defined contribution plans, post-retirement medical plans, and life insurance plans. **Source:** Towers Perrin, "Strategic Retirement Planning," 1991.

In modeling, we assume a reasonable rate of return, say 8%, and model various levels of salary and contribution as well as various ages. **Chart 2** shows several such scenarios as examples.

---

[5] It is important to model the various sources of income using a variety of employee scenarios. These scenarios should be based on the company's employee demographics and pay levels. For example, if a significant number of employees is under age 30, one of the scenarios modeled should be for an employee age 25.

FIDELITY MANAGEMENT TRUST COMPANY

$20.8 BILLION UNDER MANAGEMENT

•

Fidelity Management Trust Company

Provides Investment Management and

Client Servicing for Institutional Clients

through Separate Account Management and Commingled Pools

•

Specializing in:

EQUITIES • FIXED INCOME

HIGH INCOME BOND • INTERNATIONAL • ALTERNATIVE INVESTMENTS

RISK-CONTROLLED EQUITIES

•

For additional information, please contact:

James V. Bowhers, Senior Vice President, 617-563-7638

R. Reuel Stanley, Senior Vice President, 617-563-6529

J. David Yearwood, Senior Vice President, 617-563-6151

82 Devonshire Street, Boston, Massachusetts 02109

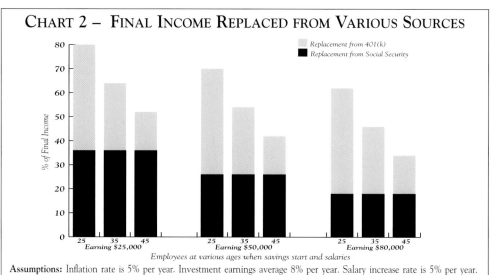

CHART 2 – FINAL INCOME REPLACED FROM VARIOUS SOURCES

Employees at various ages when savings start and salaries

Assumptions: Inflation rate is 5% per year. Investment earnings average 8% per year. Salary increase rate is 5% per year. Employee saves 6% of pay each year in the 401(k) plan. Employee begins saving at the age shown and does not take any withdrawals or loans until retirement. At retirement the 401(k) balance is used to purchase a lifetime annuity.

This modeling reveals that some employees will have more than enough retirement income from Social Security and the company DC plan, while others will not. In general, lower-paid employees who start contributing a reasonable amount to the plan at a fairly young age will have more than they need to retire comfortably. For these employees, Social Security will provide a high level of replacement income. By saving early in the company DC plan, their investments will have had a long time to build up.

In contrast, higher-paid employees who start contributing late will not have enough. Even an employee earning $50,000 a year, a not uncommon amount in high-cost areas of the country like California or the East Coast, will realize only 23% of income replacement from Social Security. A large part of retirement income for these employees must come from somewhere else.[6]

As a basic diagnostic tool, this modeling and the lessons it teaches us, are critical to help plan sponsors understand what we are and are not providing to meet our employees' retirement needs. If we aren't providing enough for some employees, the next question is, why should we care? Do we have a responsibility to do so?

MEETING EXPECTATIONS: WHY SHOULD THE PLAN SPONSOR CARE?

Providing a plan implies that its benefits will be enough, *unless something is said to the contrary.* I suspect that most employees don't worry about retirement, but tend to trust the company to provide for them when the time comes. Adequacy is, in fact, the central question for DC plans.[7] If the benefits are not adequate, the

---

[6] At Apple, we did modeling like this as part of a retirement benefits study in 1991, an outgrowth of a total compensation and benefits study. The results showed, unsurprisingly, that if employees started saving early and contributed enough, the 401(k) plan would be adequate, but employees who started saving later might not have enough to meet their retirement needs.

[7] In many respects, adequacy is in the eye of the beholder. With the shift of responsibility for investment decisions from sponsor to participant, the issue remains ambiguous. Technically, compliance with the 404(c) rules exempts the sponsor from any liability relating to inadequate retirement savings, but this is all untested ground.

employee is in for a rude awakening. Will the company stand firm at that time, risking possible liability for having implied that its benefits were adequate, when in fact the employee decides they weren't? Or will the company be forced into a legal settlement? Neither option is desirable.

There is another important reason to know whether employees will have enough to retire on when they expect to retire: employees who can't afford to retire will keep working past the point when they are most productive. If the company finds that the employee's performance is below standard, there is no graceful way for the employee to leave. The company must either manage the employee through a painful discipline process, exposing itself to possible charges of age discrimination, or buy the employee out. Neither alternative is appealing from a legal, cost, or employee relations perspective.

So we should care.

WHAT SHOULD THE COMPANY PROVIDE?

It is critical to take a step back every few years and ask ourselves what the company's philosophy is on benefits in general, and on retirement benefits in particular. By clarifying the answers to these questions, we know what we will and won't provide and why. This makes our job as plan sponsors and employee benefit communicators easier; it is also better for our employees.

This is a difficult task because most of us are so caught up in the day-to-day activities of delivering benefits that we don't give ourselves time to reflect on the "bigger" questions. At Apple, we recognized the importance of this exercise and made it a major project that lasted over a year and involved people from Compensation and Benefits, Finance, Human Resources, and other related areas. Working teams produced white papers on six topics, including the business model, the external environment, human resources objectives, the competitive standing of our compensation and benefits programs, financial projections and future trends. The findings were used to develop a set of philosophy statements for the total compensation and benefits program. These were reviewed with focus groups of managers, then refined and ultimately taken to senior management for approval in 1991.

These general philosophies could then be applied to develop more specific philosophies and strategies related to each area of benefits, including retirement and long-term capital accumulation. As a direct outgrowth of this effort, we made improvements in the Apple disability and survivor benefit plans, introduced more cost sharing into the medical plans, and improved the company matching contributions in the 401(k) plan.

As a starting point for plan sponsors who want to develop a meaningful corporate retirement philosophy, I suggest considering the following questions:

1. Should the company provide a core retirement benefit to all employees?

By "core benefits", we mean something that is automatically provided to ensure that everyone has at least a baseline of benefits protection. This question will help identify how paternalistic the company wants to be. Some companies want to provide at least some retirement benefit automatically to all employees. Others feel more comfortable letting employees choose the benefit for themselves. Of course, the downside of letting employees choose is that some may choose not to participate at all, and will later suffer the consequences. The company needs to consider how comfortable it will be then telling these employees, "It's your own fault you have no retirement income; don't expect us to fix it."

2. Should the company control the investments, or should the employees?
At issue here is the balance between paternalism and employee empowerment. Some companies feel they can maximize returns better than employees can. They cite studies showing that small investors in the stock market tend to do exactly the wrong thing: they buy a given stock when it's high; panic and sell out when it's low. Other companies whose "cultures" emphasize individual empowerment feel retirement benefits should be consistent and stress corresponding individual responsibility.

3. Should employees share in the cost? If so, to what extent?
To answer this question, the company must consider its ability to pay for retirement benefits and identify sources of funding. If the company can't afford to fund the entire plan, adequate benefits can still be provided if employees share the funding through contributions.

It's also important to consider whether the company can handle a fixed, ongoing funding commitment or whether funding should vary with company profitability.

4. What competitive position does the company want in the retirement area?
In considering this question, the company must first define who the competition is. Is it other companies in the same industry or companies of similar size and location?

Once defined, the company's benefits philosophy will give the plan sponsor a framework for deciding how much the company will provide, the degree of flexibility and choice employees will have, and how much the company should spend on the program. This makes such decisions as what type of plan to offer, the optimal design, and funding significantly easier and more appropriate to meet the company's and its employees' needs.

The guiding philosophy needs to be revisited every three to five years because answers to key questions may change over time. For instance, a small, startup company's philosophy may be that it will provide little or no retirement benefits and will only provide access for employees to make their own contributions. In an entrepreneurial stage, the company may opt for maximum choice for employees and minimal funding from the company. Five years later, however, as the company becomes more established and successful, it may find itself competing for talent from larger companies that provide more benefits. The company's philosophy will need to change to reflect its changing environment and business objectives. For Apple, our initial philosophy statements still hold up four years later, but should be reviewed in the future.

WHAT WILL EMPLOYEES GET OUT OF THE DC PLAN?

The next step is to take a closer look at how employees are using the plan. For example, if participation is optional, how many employees are not participating? Who are they in terms of age, salary, company location and other demographics and why aren't they participating? Which employees aren't contributing enough to receive the maximum company matching contributions? This information helps identify employees who might not have enough retirement savings later on.

In companies where participation is less than desired, it is often a common mis-

take to assume that it's the lower-paid employees who can't afford to contribute. At Apple, we learned from our initial survey of non-participants that the most common reason for not contributing was "can't afford to." However, we found no correlation with pay; in some cases, the employees who claimed they couldn't afford to contribute were earning $80,000 or more a year! We found employees in the manufacturing plant earning $25,000 a year who were contributing the maximum. The real reason was clearly something else.

What we needed to do was identify the gap between employees' perceptions, expectations and reality. For example, if the DC plan cannot provide enough to employees in certain scenarios, do employees know that? Or do they expect the company to provide what they need in the event of a shortfall?

To understand what's really going on, the most revealing methods are to conduct surveys and focus groups. There is no substitute for getting out of the office and listening to what employees are saying. We found the results were enlightening, even surprising.

Some employees, like the $80,000 per year earners, don't contribute because they overestimate the reduction in pay that results from participating in the plan. The solution was to show them how tax advantages reduce impact on net take-home pay and give them some basic education on setting financial goals and budgeting.

Other employees don't contribute because they haven't gotten around to enrolling. These employees need to hear about the effects of long-term buildup and understand the dramatic consequences between early, rather than later, savings. Lack of participation may also indicate that the enrollment process is too cumbersome.

Some employees don't contribute because they are confused about what funds to invest in. These employees need to be educated about how various investment vehicles can meet their individual needs.

Some employees aren't contributing enough, but think they are. These employees need to do some personal modeling to figure out how much they should be saving.

Still other employees invest their money in the lowest-risk option because they believe it's the "safest." They need to understand more about investment risk vs. retirement risk and the consequence of losing ground against the pounding impact of inflation.

KEY MESSAGES

There are some basic messages that all employees need to hear. The most important of all is the company's philosophy for providing the plan. Why does it provide the plan? What level of commitment does it have to employees? Is the plan intended to help retain employees for their entire career, or simply be part of employees' ongoing savings plans?

The message needs to be balanced and honest. If the company can't afford to provide for all employees' needs, it should say so. How can you do this without detracting from the plan? One way is to explain it in its business context. For example:

"Chips, Inc. is a young, growing company with high startup costs. In such a volatile environment, it doesn't make sense to make the long-term commitment to a traditional retirement plan with the resulting fixed-cost commitment. On the other hand, Chips is concerned about its employees over the long term, and we

YOUR EMPLOYEES MAY NOT BE ACCUSTOMED TO THE SERVICE WE PROVIDE. BUT THEY COULD GET USED TO IT.

DREYFUS GROUP
RETIREMENT PLANS

For more information about our full range
of Defined Contribution Plan services, call:
Robert W. Stone
Executive Vice President
(212) 922-6110

want to provide you with the opportunity to save for the future, wherever it may take you. As a result, we offer our employees a 401(k) plan and, at this time, we are increasing the company matching contributions to help your savings grow faster."

Here's another approach:

"Big Utility provides a retirement income plan which, along with Social Security, provides basic retirement income for all employees who make a career at Big. We believe that if you stay at Big for your entire career, you should be able to retire with some income in addition to Social Security. However, to maintain your standard of living in retirement, you will need additional savings. In this area, Big will partner with you. Big provides a 401(k) plan and will match your contributions, but you need to decide if you want to contribute and if so, how much. This is a personal matter, and every employee is different. To help you decide, there are educational tools available..."

Both of these examples balance the good news that employees want to hear ("we're giving you a benefit") with the news that they might not want to hear ("but it can't provide everything"). When employees are told the truth and given the reasons, there is acceptance and appreciation rather than surprise and disappointment when the bad news is delivered the hard way.

It's important to note that not all employees need to hear the same messages. For example, some employees need basic education on their long-term needs and on the advantages of pre-tax contributions. The employees who aren't participating need to understand why they need to, how to start small, and how to compute the effect on their paycheck. In contrast, the employees who are already contributing will be bored by such basic information; they are ready to hear more about different types of investments, diversifying a portfolio and designing an investment strategy. The chart below shows some examples of key messages and who needs to hear them.

KEY MESSAGE	WHO NEEDS TO HEAR IT
You need to save now for your future	Non-participating employees who don't know why; those who know why but continue to procrastinate
You can afford to save	Non-participants
There are tax advantages	Higher income employees; low-level or non-participants
Concepts of risk and return	Employees invested in low-risk funds only
Why diversification is important	Employees invested in only one fund
Types of investments	Intermediate investors hungry for more investment education
Portfolio management philosophies	Advanced investors
Up-to-date performance information	Advanced investors

While not everyone can or needs to become an advanced investor, the company objective should be to meet everyone's need for information and move those below the "intermediate" level up the knowledge curve. To do this, plan communications need to address individuals at their present level, and then bring them along to where they need to be.

RETHINKING COMMUNICATIONS

Employee benefits legislation and regulations tell us the basic requirements for communicating the DC plans, and the plan sponsors I know are generally in compliance. Most companies exert great effort to produce a traditional benefits handbook and, if we want the protections of 404(c), we distribute prospectuses for each investment option as well.[8] But somehow, employees still aren't getting all the information they need. Clearly, we need to go beyond these standard, required forms of communication if we want employees to really understand opportunities available to them.

It helps to look more closely at traditional communications vehicles, define the purpose they serve and assess their success in achieving their goals. For example, the benefits handbook is usually a factual presentation of the plan features, including information on how it works and how to enroll. Most employees won't read it cover to cover, but will use it for reference when they need a specific question answered. The prospectus for an individual fund also presents basic facts about that fund: its investment philosophy, the underlying investments and past performance. Yet neither of these vehicles answers the three main questions employees are asking:

- ➤ **What should I do?**
- ➤ **Why is this good for me?**
- ➤ **Why should I care?**
- ➤ **Does it matter?**

It's clear that the "one size fits all" approach to benefits communications doesn't work. Employees need to be able to get the information they need easily and quickly. This implies that different vehicles or forms of communications are, in fact, necessary.

FROM COMMUNICATIONS TO EDUCATION

My mother always critiqued my writing by saying, "Don't tell me, show me." In the benefits handbook style of communications we've all been guilty of telling employees about the plan instead of showing how it can work for them. "Showing" is a much more effective way to educate employees who are getting information and being asked to make critical choices that can, and probably will, influence their lives in a substantial way. Education works best when information

---

[8] Proposed 404(c) regulations introduced in 1993 specify that plan fiduciaries can be protected from liability for DC plan losses if they meet certain requirements. Those requirements include offering at least three investment alternatives with varying risk/return characteristics, providing frequent and thorough communications on those alternatives, and allowing participants to transfer money among them frequently.

is presented initially through multiple media (printed material, lectures, graphics). Learning can then be reinforced as employees actively work through the information on their own using available resources for answers to specific questions.

In a company setting, it's possible to use multiple media without huge expense or effort. One approach is to provide print information in shorter formats (small booklets or paycheck stuffers), each focusing on one aspect of the plan. For example, one could deal with the philosophy and general design of the plan; the next could describe basic investment concepts, and so on. With more concise information, employees are more likely to understand the key messages before losing interest or becoming confused.

BEYOND PRINT

Although using print media is a good beginning, it can be supplemented successfully with periodic employee meetings, brown bag lunches, or video presentations. Such events can be led by outside vendors, financial planners, investment managers, company benefits staff or people trained by the benefits staff. We have found it very effective to run employee meetings using a team approach. A member of the benefits staff explains how the plan works and someone from the investment management company explains the funds.

It can be tempting to run meetings using financial planners. On average, I get several calls a week from financial planners willing to come on-site to do meetings at no charge to the company. The problem is, of course, there is no free lunch. Generally, those offering to speak for "free" make commissions from any financial products they sell, and therefore may not be unbiased in their recommendations. By allowing outside representatives to come on-site, the company implies endorsement. I prefer to pay consulting experts who don't sell products. At Apple, we have had good results working with an outside consultant on an ongoing basis. She learned about the company's culture, objectives, and benefit plans, and could handle a broad range of questions as a result.

Field locations can prove to be a special challenge. Without someone on-site to explain the plan and help employees enroll, simply mailing out printed material may not be enough. It may be more effective to train line supervisors and give them materials to help them run meetings. At Apple we have found this approach particularly effective, especially in reaching employees on the evening or night shifts.

One way to reinforce the messages through active learning is to provide workshops with workbooks on budgeting, establishing a personal financial plan, setting financial goals, and working towards those goals. For example, Hewlett Packard provides workshops that last a full Saturday and require both preparatory work and the completion of a workbook at the session. The sessions are conducted by an outside company with expertise in this area. HP subsidizes most of the cost, but requires a small fee from employees as a way to ensure their commitment to the process. They have received excellent feedback from employees who have completed the workshops.

A way to promote active learning in a less labor-intensive way is to provide interactive software tools for employees. These allow employees to go at their own pace and access the information they need as they need it. They are also personal; since the employee enters his or her own data, the results are customized. If an

METLIFE USES A POSITIVE EDUCATIONAL FOCUS TO EXPLAIN 401(K)
RETIREMENT PLANNING. OUR GOAL-ORIENTED, "YOU-CAN-DO-IT"
TONE IS ENCOURAGING. OUR FLEXIBLE ENROLLMENT MATERIALS
ARE THOROUGH YET EASY TO UNDERSTAND. AND OUR
NATIONAL NETWORK OF EXPERIENCED ENROLLMENT
TEAMS INSTILL A COMFORT AND CONFIDENCE
LEVEL THAT EQUIPS PARTICIPANTS TO
MAKE BETTER DECISIONS. THE
RESULT? QUALITY PLAN
ENROLLMENTS.

A 401(K) PLAN
THAT'S EASY FOR
EMPLOYEES TO
UNDERSTAND

METLIFE IS A FULL-SERVICE, SINGLE-SOURCE PROVIDER OF CUSTOM DEFINED CONTRIBUTION PLANS. FOR MORE
INFORMATION ABOUT OUR PARTICIPATION AND SERVICE GUARANTEE, CALL GARY LINEBERRY AT 1-212-578-3181.

EDUCATE
COMMUNICATE

MetLife®
Defined Contribution Group

Metropolitan Life Insurance Company
One Madison Avenue, New York, NY 10010-3690

940610D(0695)MLIC-LD

employee is not saving enough to retire at the desired age, the software model will show it. With the graphic and multimedia features now available on desktop computers, interactive software can be both easy and fun for employees to use. Computer "kiosks" can be set up in strategic locations around the company if the programs aren't available to all employees at their desktops.

Apple developed a stand-alone software package that employees use for modeling and enrolling in the plan. After entering their pay and proposed contribution percentage, the software calculates the tax advantage, total contributions, and company matching contributions for a year. It will also project savings buildup over time, and will do projections of retirement income replacement. Employees can play with the modeling as long as they like, and print out various scenarios. When they've decided how much to contribute, the software will print out the enrollment form for them to sign and send in.

This software was developed in less than three months and at a fraction of the cost for comparable printed brochures and workbooks. Employees can get at just the information they want, and it's easier than using a workbook, because the calculations are done by the software. The experience is fun, easy, and non-threatening and the person comes away having learned and accomplished something important and worthwhile.

I have had the opportunity to talk about and demonstrate our software package to various groups of benefits professionals, and someone invariably asks, "Can we buy that? Would Apple sell the software?" The answer is no; Apple is not in the applications business. In any case, the software we've developed is tailored to the Apple plan and would need to be modified for another company. The large benefits consulting companies all have systems experts who can help other companies design a similarly useful software tool.

The advent of electronic mail creates an incredible opportunity for companies to distribute information quickly and update it often. At Apple we post daily fund values and past fund performance on our e-mail bulletin board where our advanced investors can access it whenever they choose. Plan announcements and updates can also be posted quickly.

The timing of various communications is just as important as their format and content. Experience has taught us that most people don't pay attention to something until they need it. This leads to the concept of "just in time" training. The most effective DC communications are those that are in hand when employees are thinking about the subject. This is why we combined modeling functions in the same software that employees use to enroll. Another possibility is to enclose a brief newsletter with the quarterly statement. Our surveys show that the newsletter gets high marks because it isn't too long, and employees are inclined to read it because they are already thinking about the plan while looking at their current statement.

Another way to look at communications is from an *event-centered* standpoint. As plan sponsors, we tend to think of benefits as individual plans and communicate them that way. But employees approach benefits from a life event or situation perspective; at that moment they want to know how all their benefits apply to that situation.

One of the best times to capture an employee's attention is the moment of hire. The pressures of the job haven't set in yet and employees know that they need to do something about their benefits. This is a unique opportunity to communicate essentials. But the opportunity will be lost if we inundate new employees with too many benefits booklets and forms once they have actually begun working.

At Apple we used to give a two-hour, stand-up presentation on benefits for new hires as part of a lengthy employee orientation program. The feedback we got was that some employees understood benefits and were bored through most of the presentation, while others didn't get enough detail.

In response, we developed a self-paced interactive software tool that gives basic benefits information in modules so the individual using it can access only the information desired. The tool also gives help for making decisions in several ways. Video clips of employees talking about what they chose and why work well for employees who relate to examples. One video clip shows an employee saying "I'm a single parent, so it's real important for me to save for the future education of my children. That's why I save the maximum in the 401(k) plan." The software also includes analytic tools for choosing life insurance or other benefits. Because of the excellent development tools available, this software was developed in two months at a cost of only $10,000.

After trying different forms of communications, we realized that no one form of communications addresses all our needs. We get the best results from repeating the same messages in different ways and through different media. Some media (short booklets and employee meetings) work better for beginning investors. Newsletters target both beginning and intermediate investors. Interactive software spans beginning, intermediate and advanced levels because it is self-paced and users can access information they want and skip information that is too basic or too advanced.

How do we know it's working? One indication is that plan participation has increased and employees who participate are well diversified among the investment funds. Another indication is that employees are asking for more financial education and other investment vehicles they can utilize through payroll deduction. This tells me that employees get the message that the 401(k) plan may not be enough since, increasingly, they are asking for something more.

PULLING IT ALL TOGETHER

As DC plan sponsors, we have put more of the control and responsibility for saving for the future in the hands of our employees. This means we have a responsibility to give them the tools and information they need to make informed decisions. I have outlined the road map we follow to ensure we fulfill that responsibility. Following it means sponsors must clarify what they are and aren't providing, learn what employees think, where the gaps are, and then develop the best ways to fill them. In the end, we will have developed a closer partnership and a more productive, responsive relationship with our employees.

➤ Develop a clear company philosophy on retirement benefits. This will help you clarify how much you want to provide, and in what form.

➤ Evaluate your current DC plan along with any other plans to determine how close they come to meeting employee needs for adequate retirement income.

➤ Analyze current plan participation. Find out the demographics of employees who don't participate and those of employees who participate but don't diversify their investment mix. Slice and dice the data until you zero in on who they are. This will help you develop effective strategies for reaching non- or low-level participants.

➤ Review communications materials. Are they delivering the key messages in clear, understandable and actionable ways? Are they targeting the employees who need to hear?

➤ Use a multi-media approach. Different people learn in different ways.

➤ Consider interactive tools like computer software for employee desktops or in a kiosk arrangement.

➤ *Above all, be honest.* If the company can't provide everything to every employee, tell them. Clarify and define reasonable, realistic expectations. Employees can then find other ways to meet their savings needs.

*S*ince its inception in 1993, 404(c)[1] has stirred considerable debate in the DC plan world. Applauded by some benefits administrators for designating what many view as minimum requirements and greater flexibility, it is criticized by others for its cumbersome communications requirements and confusing ambiguities. Misconceptions about fiduciary responsibility, consequent liability and available protection abound.

The debate is hardly academic. Although technically the rule is voluntary, many legal experts are skeptical. In addition, some plan sponsors perceive 404(c) as offering "a safe harbor;" in fact, it does not. Perhaps most troubling is the confusion over education. Since DC plans transfer investment responsibility to participants who are, in most cases, inexperienced investors, employers wonder if they will cross the invisible line that separates education from advice; they worry about sponsor liability if participants suffer losses as a result of misleading education information. Unease prevails as the only clear message to plan sponsors is: watch your step.

Extensive research in the preparation of **A Wing and A Prayer** confirms the absence of a consensus on the interpretation of 404(c) throughout the DC industry. Efforts to comply with the regulation are marked by a myriad of questions; a clear

---

[1] ERISA section 404(c) is a voluntary rule designed to offer protection to plan sponsors of individually directed benefit accounts from liability due to losses resulting from participants' investment decisions.

To qualify for protection plan sponsors must fulfill three basic requirements: (1) offer participants a minimum of three fund options (excluding a company stock fund) which span the risk/reward spectrum; (2) provide for individual control of the assets, and enable the participants to switch among these options with a frequency related to their volatility (at a minimum, once per quarter); (3) provide communications materials about plan investment options, how to implement them, and who manages them. Plan sponsors are responsible for designing the plan; determining what investment alternatives will be offered and their quality; and selecting investment managers. Plan sponsors retain ultimate fiduciary responsibility, as defined by ERISA.

shared understanding is elusive, at best. Consistent with our goal to educate our readers on all issues of compelling concern to them, Investors Press includes this **Special 404(c) Report** in an effort to lift the veil of confusion that clouds interpretation of this regulation.

In **Part I** authors Nathaniel Duffield, Sally Gottlieb and Rita Metras exchange their personal views about the rule, discuss its strengths and weaknesses and describe their companies' responses to it. None professes to be an expert on 404(c) or on the complex 1974 ERISA statute to which it is appended; their conversation illustrates a range of DC and overall pension plan designs that gives readers a sampling of plan sponsor responses to the rule. Their comments also reflect a clear division of opinion between benefits/human resources and investment administrators.

Part II features comments from a senior DOL spokesman (an attorney instrumental in writing the regulation who remains unidentified at the DOL's request); ERISA attorney Luke Bailey, who has written extensively on 404(c) and whose clients are predominantly DC plan sponsors; and Brian Schaefer, president of a firm that develops customized communication and education programs for DC plans. These industry experts exchange opinions on the following points of greatest ambiguity in 404(c) interpretation:

> ➤ How voluntary is the rule?
> ➤ Is 404(c) a "safe harbor" regulation?
> ➤ Is education required of plan sponsors for compliance?

Our three ERISA experts concur that because many areas of ERISA have never been clarified in case law, some perspective is in order and a wave of legal contests will likely build over the next several years. Clarity and consensus on 404(c) interpretation is in the future. For now, everyone will have to wait and see — prudently.

PART I: DUFFIELD, GOTTLIEB & METRAS

Q. *Does your fund comply? If not, why not? Can you envision a situation where the fund would not comply?*

DUFFIELD: We were close to compliance, so we completed the remaining requirements. But the protection that 404(c) gives is fairly limited. The fact is that plan sponsors, fiduciaries, are still responsible for making sure the investment choices they offer are prudently structured. Regardless of how prudently you are structured, however, if you have two investment choices, 404(c) doesn't prevent you from being nailed.

The problem is that 404(c), even though voluntary, may establish a standard for DC plans. A disgruntled plan participant, for example, could go to an attorney familiar with 404(c) requirements, which could lead to court action, despite whether compliance was voluntary.

METRAS: For us it was a fiduciary decision, since we were planning to increase our DC investments and had already begun to expand our communications effort.

Why wouldn't a company comply? If the DC plan were a company stock fund, by its very nature it couldn't comply. If you only offer the

RETIREMENT PAYOUT DAY: YEAR 2019

required three investment choices without significant communications, you're on shaky ground. The requirement for prospectuses is curious, considering few people read them and they are expensive to mail. If costs are too great, companies may decide against compliance.

GOTTLIEB: For us it was an easy decision; we were in compliance with just about all the provisions. All we had to do was add a statement on all our communications that we intended to comply.

Q. *What impact, if any, has 404(c) had on your fund choices?*

GOTTLIEB: None. When the regulation came out we already had six funds with varying risk/return characteristics. The regulation requires quarterly transfers and we were already on daily transfers.

METRAS: We had already made our three new fund choices. 404(c) gave us an implementation date to shoot for.

DUFFIELD: None.

Q. *Has the rule impacted your communications effort?*

GOTTLIEB: It caused us to review everything: plan design, communications and administrative rules. But it was really a non-issue for us since we already exceeded the requirements.

METRAS: Since we were either doing or intended to do most of the communications items, just a few things had to be added, including a statement acknowledging our intention to comply.

NCM Capital ...

On Equity Investing

"As a value manager, we believe that the security selection process begins with the identification of securities with low relative price earnings ratios."

In the seven years since its founding, NCM Capital Management Group, Inc. has attracted a client base of some 70 employee benefit, foundation and endowment plans. With nearly $3 billion under management NCM Capital is one of the nation's most successful and well-respected minority owned investment advisory firms.

The firm offers a breadth of investment options which include equity, fixed income and balanced portfolio management. In all of its disciplines, the

On Fixed Income

"We believe that weighting corporates, particularly in the industrial and finance sectors, will add value to our portfolios."

Maceo K. Sloan,
Chairman, President and CEO

firm seeks to exceed respective index returns over a market cycle while maintaining a low risk profile. Additionally, it is the firm's goal to set the industry standard for client service.

To receive a detailed description of NCM Capital's investment processes or additional information on how the firm can help you meet your own investment objectives, please phone or write:

Marc V. Reid
Tel (919) 688-0620
Fax (919) 683-1352

NCM Capital
Management Group, Inc.
103 West Main Street
Durham, NC 27701-3638

DUFFIELD: Only slightly, because we were almost overcomplying with communications.

Q. What is the most important requirement or provision of the rule?

METRAS: The DOL's emphasis on giving employees enough information to make informed decisions. Some companies just gave the facts about their investment funds, without education. People need to know how to apply the facts to reach their retirement savings goals.

DUFFIELD: What's significant is the idea of government stepping in and saying what's in the best interests of the plan participants' investments. I don't agree with three funds as a minimum number of offerings to cover the risk/return spectrum. A good capital accumulation plan can be structured with two choices. You'd have to think a long time to find ways to improve on the two funds we originally offered. It's really a matter of how well a portfolio is structured.

Some companies have gone overboard increasing fund choices to 30 or 40. That many choices is more confusing than beneficial to participants.

GOTTLIEB: All three aspects of the rule — the range of investment options, the asset transfer provision and communications are equally important. All go hand in glove.

This rule makes a lot of sense, which is unusual. If you have a well-designed DC plan, you're already there.

Q. Education vs. advice: does 404(c) clarify the distinction legally?

GOTTLIEB AND METRAS: No it doesn't; so this is still an area where plan sponsors need to be careful and use good judgment.

DUFFIELD: 404(c) does not clarify the distinction, and that is a problem. In a recent interview,[2] Assistant Secretary Olena Berg of the DOL discussed how you avoid crossing the line. But her comments were vague; she indicated that education programs should be kept generic. She also said that if the investment provider is also the education provider, it is a potential conflict of interest that could destroy the protections 404(c) offers. She implied that although you might use an outside firm to provide education, you still have the duty to monitor it. And if you think you're complying with 404(c) and you hire an unqualified firm to provide education — you might have a problem.

Q. What's wrong with 404(c)?

GOTTLIEB: Nothing really. I don't wait for the law to tell me everything I have to do. The regulations I have trouble with are those that are tremendously detailed. This regulation is more general; they gave us the framework and the philosophy, and then gave us the leeway to look at the spirit and intent of the law. We can figure out the best way to comply without being bound by lots of dictates.

---

[2] Defined Contribution News, April 18, 1994, p. 1.

METRAS: The DOL did a good job incorporating employer input. We've been living and working with it. My only question is, again: how valuable are prospectuses to participants?

DUFFIELD: One problem is the insufficient guidelines on communications. Some of Olena Berg's comments raise more questions than they answer. Most plan sponsors want to have a good communications program but have to walk on eggshells to be sure they're not raising any legal problems.

Another thing about 404(c) that's tough: it's somewhat transaction-oriented. You can make every effort to comply but if something happens that doesn't comply with one little aspect, you don't have any protection. Say, for instance, you've distributed information on the plan as required but it accidentally wasn't mailed to one plan participant. This person says "you didn't provide this communication to me before I made my choice." Thus, for that participant, and that transaction, you probably couldn't claim protection. When you have 60,000 participants as we do, it may be difficult to prove beyond a shadow of a doubt that you provided what you were supposed to.

PART II: DOL, BAILEY & SCHAEFER

Q. Why is the rule voluntary? What if a plan sponsor chooses not to comply?

DOL: Congress, by statute, envisioned that it would be voluntary. 404(c) is just an available mechanism for people who would otherwise be responsible to be exempt from liability in exchange for certain provisions. Remember, you don't have to offer a private pension plan. It's an optional business decision.

If you want to offer your employees the chance to direct their own accounts, this rule enables you to do so without being responsible for their investment decisions. We have no way of knowing the degree of compliance; my sense is that most plans that provide self-directed accounts are complying.

SCHAEFER: It's only voluntary now. If problems persist or loom large later on, it will become mandatory.

BAILEY: There is a lot of misunderstanding about how voluntary the rule really is. Certainly, you don't have to have a plan that offers participants investment choices. But if you do give choices, there's no clear answer to what happens if you don't comply with the 404(c) regulations. Many plan sponsors are not comfortable with the uncertainty and feel compelled to comply.

If you give choices but don't comply, and an employee sues for losses in his or her account, *and the plan was not 404(c) compliant*, then probably your only defense would be "substantive prudence." If it turns out the account was prudently invested you'd be okay, despite not complying with 404(c). Otherwise, you'd probably not be safe.

If nothing else, 404(c) protects you from a participant's imprudent asset allocation and timing decisions. So, if you decide to give the participant choices that can lead to unwise decisions which, I will note, is a very interesting premise from both the policy and plan design standpoints, then I think you should not consider 404(c) voluntary and comply.

There is a school of thought that says: "If we don't meet the regulation, we can't claim it as defense. But our overall plan design and structure of participant choices is reasonable, so a judge wouldn't hold us responsible for the participant's "mistakes." While this makes sense, it's difficult to square with the 404(c) regulations' explicit statement that compliance with them is the exclusive means of avoiding liability for losses based on an argument that the participant chose his or her own investments.

Q. Many are confused about whether 404(c) is "a safe harbor." Is it?

BAILEY: 404(c) is NOT "a safe harbor," although many people wish it were. A "safe harbor" regulation is one in which the regulatory agency carves out the clearest cases and says if you comply with these, you'll definitely be protected. But you are also permitted to take your chances and demonstrate compliance with the statute based on "facts and circumstances."

With 404(c), the DOL says something different: *you must meet every requirement of the regulation* — otherwise you have no 404(c) protection.

Q. Is education a requirement of 404(c)?

BAILEY: I don't think the DOL intended to imply that a plan sponsor would have any obligation to provide education, as opposed to prospectus-like fund disclosures, which of course, are required. Just think what would have happened if they had tried. They simply could not have outlined guidelines for a standard education program or education requirement without

Two Million Employees Won't Have To Settle For Just A Gold Watch

Delaware knows what people need when they plan their retirement: information and guidance to set goals and the investment options to help them reach the comfortable retirement they dream about.

With $26 billion under management and 60 years of investment experience, Delaware is a proven industry leader. In fact, the future financial security of 2 million employees has been entrusted to our management through the pension funds of some of the largest companies in the country.

The quality of your company's 401(k) retirement plan lets your employees know how important they are to you. If your employees deserve more than a gold watch when they retire, it's time to consider *Delaware*.

**DELAWARE
MANAGEMENT
COMPANY, INC.**

Minette van Noppen
Vice President
215-751-2910

exposing themselves to a tidal wave of industry criticism, given the lack of unanimity on investment theories, the open-endedness of the subject and the compliance burden that a good education program might entail.

Some lawyers even question whether "education" is desirable. If the sponsor brings in someone to provide education, does it risk incurring the very liability it sought to avoid by complying with 404(c)?

I believe there are important Human Resources benefits to investment education, and that any liability risk is manageable. But from a strictly legal perspective, if the sponsor clearly met 404(c)'s requirements — which again, simply don't include investment education — then that should be sufficient to avoid liability.

Q. Education vs. advice: does 404(c) clarify the distinction legally?

DOL: The 404(c) rules do not clarify what is or isn't advice. That is dealt with under Section 3(21) of ERISA. To render investment advice under the regulation, you must meet several requirements: being in the business of providing such advice, doing so for a fee, providing information that is particularized. If plan sponsors provide only education they are not setting themselves up for trouble. The bottom line is it's not that easy to consider something "investment advice."

SCHAEFER: No, 404(c) doesn't clarify the distinction but it should. If you make a sincere, honest effort to educate employees, you really should not have any liability.

What employees need is education: process information, not just product information. They can understand what's in the fund, but not why they should put money into it. They need the confidence to invest, and process information helps them build confidence.

BAILEY: Although other ERISA provisions address this somewhat, nothing addresses it specifically in the 404(c) context except the somewhat oblique prohibition in the 404(c) regulation against "improper influence."

Let's consider this gray area: suppose you offer your plan through a brokerage firm that has a program that effectively turns every participant's account into a wrap account. Assume your plan is otherwise in perfect compliance with 404(c). The brokerage offers individual counseling based on individual investor profiles. So the way the participants' money ultimately is invested depends on this other relationship that may not even be regulated by ERISA but may instead legally be an investment adviser, regulated by federal and state securities laws. The legal status of the adviser is unclear under ERISA, because it's unclear who is being advised. Is the advice provided to the plan or to the participant? Remember, under 404(c) the participant is not a fiduciary for his own account and presumably has no authority himself to appoint a fiduciary. This is a major question, one that hasn't been addressed comprehensively by most plan sponsors or service providers.

Q. *In a recent interview in <u>Defined Contribution News</u>, Olena Berg endorsed generic employee education programs. She commented on the possible "undue influence" of education materials provided by a DC plan's mutual fund provider and suggested that such an arrangement may hinder a plan's ability to assume protection under 404(c). What's your response?*

DOL: Say you're a mutual fund provider and you offer four different pooled investment vehicles to a client. In one of them, you net 1% of returns, on another .50%. There's an incentive to skew the communications to encourage investment where you'd net 1% vs. .50% of returns. We don't want someone with a financial interest in what participants choose advising them about fund selection. The potential for abuse is so great. An impartial party should provide these kinds of educational communications.

Q. *What legal risk does the employer face if it decides to provide investment education?*

BAILEY: Suppose a suit is brought by a participant in connection with losses he claims resulted directly from the employer's alleged misleading investment education.

The source of any legal liability (to the extent the plan sponsor, and not the "educator," is the defendant) would probably be ERISA, and for technical reasons, the suit would probably be for breach of fiduciary duty. How could the plaintiff frame this case successfully? Even if you could somehow argue that the investment educator was a fiduciary who committed a breach (a doubtful strategy), it still defies the fundamental provision of 404(c): if the plan complied with 404(c), no fiduciary is liable "for any loss or by reason of any breach" resulting from the participant's exercise of control.

The only valid line of attack for the plaintiff where the plan otherwise complied with 404(c) would seem to be that he or she was subjected to "improper influence," which the regulations do specifically state negate 404(c) protection.

So the plaintiff would have to argue the misleading investment education amounted to "improper influence." That could turn out to be a high hurdle.

Even if "improper influence" could be established as the basis for loss of 404(c) protection, fiduciary liability is *not automatic*. The plan sponsor could attempt to prove procedural prudence (did the fiduciary carefully examine the investment direction, the educator's credentials and the course of study?); then attempt to prove substantive prudence (regardless of the procedure, was the portfolio composition prudent?).

A plan sponsor that's serious about education would be well advised to do some of the same "due diligence" with the education provider as it would do with an investment manager in a traditional non-participant-directed plan.

Bosto
Mellon wou
make a ver
announcer

Mellon Trust

n Safe and
ld like to
y powerful
nent.

We are now Mellon Trust. One force. United in
philosophy, resources and expertise. In a bold move, two of
the most respected names in institutional trust have been
joined under a new banner. Reaffirming our commitment to
technology, flexibility, quality service and an unmatched
system of financial reporting and analysis. Call Mellon Trust
at 1-800-419-4501. And put our energy to work for you.

Nominated by his peers and chosen by Investors Press for his innovative thinking and outstanding contributions to his profession, the following Trailblazer has been honored as one of our 1994 Award Winners. We take great pleasure in sharing his accomplishments with you.

STEPHEN L. FORDHAM

Division Manager –
Corporate Benefits
A T & T

What do you get when you mix Marine discipline with Principle-Centered Leadership and evangelical zeal? Steve Fordham's swift, record-setting rise through the ranks at Southern Bell and his similarly impressive decade-long performance (1983-1993) in compensation and benefits at AT&T.

Today, Fordham is applying his impressive managerial skills to his latest challenge: only 17 months after taking the helm of AT&T's 230,000-participant DC program, he has orchestrated a major plan conversion for AT&T's Long-Term Savings Plan for Management Employees. Its 118,000 participants will gain a new recordkeeper, daily valuation and an expanded roster of ten investment options.

It's not just the monumental size of the conversion that's significant. Although outsourcing half of AT&T's total DC plan participants was a politically sensitive undertaking, it was driven by Fordham's unwavering commitment to "quality with a small 'q' " (rather than to "Total Quality Management") — in this case, determining and fulfilling customer needs. (Participants in the union-negotiated Long Term Savings and Security Plan and a frozen ESOP will continue with in-house recordkeeping).

From focus groups to informal feedback, the message was clear: participants wanted more funds and features like daily valuation that the in-house recordkeeping system simply couldn't provide. The prospect of cost-sharing was not a deterrent.

Employee interest in expanded options, added to management's concern about the insufficient diversification of participant portfolios, drove the decision to double investment options from five to ten. According to Fordham, only three months before conversion the $9 billion in the management plan was divided equally among company stock, the GIC fund and the remaining three options. Besides the company stock fund and reconfigured fixed income and equity funds, new offerings include an international fund, three pre-mixed (lifecycle) funds and three mutual funds. "My preference was to give even more choices," says Fordham, "but this expansion is already a big step." Coupled with a superior match (4% to the employees' maximum 6% contribution, vs. the 3% industry average), the revised plan seems all the more promising.

Three months before conversion, participants received an investment guide designed to help them understand investment basics and encourage their utilizing the full range of available investment options. But the guide, newsletters, even the electronic bulletin board, aren't enough, according to Fordham. To meet the challenge of providing useful education tools to a huge, demographically diverse workforce, Fordham rigorously screened and carefully handpicked three outside education providers.

Fordham's efforts embody his prized "Plan Principles." This manifesto, which took his 13-member team seven months to draft, articulates the plan's purpose and goals. Paramount among them is fostering a greater sense of individual responsibility among participants for their retirement savings.

While the results remain to be seen, Fordham's ambition is to have a plan conversion that is *dead solid perfect... Who* knows whether or not I'm a Trailblazer. What I *really* strive to be is a very good professional manager."

RESOURCE GUIDE

*T*HE INVESTORS PRESS RESOURCE GUIDE IS A SERIES OF SPECIAL SECTIONS INTENDED TO ENHANCE THE EDUCATIONAL VALUE OF THIS BOOK AND EXTEND ITS USEFULNESS AS A REFERENCE TOOL AND RESOURCE.

➤ UNDERWRITERS' PROFILES

➤ ANNOTATED BIBLIOGRAPHY

➤ GLOSSARY

➤ AUTHORS' BIOGRAPHIES

UNDERWRITER PROFILES

Angelo, Gordon & Co.

245 Park Avenue, New York, NY 10167
Phone: 212-692-2042 • Fax: 212-867-9328

Key Contact Information:
John M. Angelo, *Chief Executive Officer*
Michael L. Gordon, *Chief Operating Officer*
Marsha P. Roth, *Managing Director*

Year Founded:	1988

Total assets under management:	$600 Million

Minimum account size:	$25 Million (individual)
	$1 Million (commingled)

Assets managed by client category:

	ASSETS MANAGED *(in millions)*
Corporate Funds	$150
Foundations & Endowments	75
Individuals	375

Special areas of expertise:
Non-traditional investment strategies in bankruptcy, distressed real estate, risk arbitrage, convertible hedging, utility hedging or their combinations.

Investment Approach:
Angelo, Gordon offers corporate plan sponsors an expertise in creating absolute returns that utilize combinations of risk arbitrage, bankruptcy and distressed real estate. Additionally, the Firm seeks to generate a multiple of the Treasury rate by utilizing convertible bond hedging and/or a long/short electric utility strategy. The common thread that links all these investments is little or no correlation to stock or bond markets to limit downside risk. The implementation of these strategies is a conservative evaluation approach generated through in-depth research and a diversification strategy applied within each portfolio.

Barings

High Street Tower, 125 High Street, Suite 2700
Boston, MA 02110
Phone: 617-951-0052 • Fax: 617-951-1376

Key Contact Information:
Peter S. Hartley	
Managing Director (US)	617-951-0052
M. Fraser Blakely	
Director, Marketing	617-951-0052

Year Founded:
International management:	1979
Domestic management:	1967

Total tax-exempt assets under management from all sources:
Worldwide	$44.4 Billion
North American based clients	10.9 Billion

Special areas of expertise:
Barings is a multi-dimensional, global asset management company specializing in global, international, regional and single country equity and fixed income management for clients worldwide.

Frequency of reporting results:	Quarterly

Assets managed by client category:
(As relates to North American based clients only as of 3/31/94)

	NO. OF CLIENTS	ASSETS ($ millions)
Corporates	48	$4689.6
Consultants	7	237.1
Publics	18	3242.1
Endowments	15	304.4
Foundations	7	421.5
Other	25	2035.8
Total	**120**	**10,930.5**

Investment approach:
• Top-down, centralized asset allocation
• Bottom-up, fundamental security selection
Barings' ultimate equity strategy is to find growing economies and companies at the right local valuation. Senior Asset Allocation Specialists formulate policy based on original research conducted by Regional Specialist teams located worldwide. Primary considerations for the equity process at both the country and stock levels are earnings growth, valuations and liquidity. Barings' fixed income process focuses on high sustainable real returns while controlling credit and currency risk.

Chancellor Capital Management, Inc.

1166 Avenue of the Americas, New York, NY 10036
Phone: 212-278-9000 • Fax: 212-278-9544

Key Contact Information:
Nina Lesavoy, *Head of Client Service*
and New Business Development   212-278-9664

Year founded:
1896; *an employee owned firm since April 1992*

**Total assets under
management from all sources:** $27.8 Billion*

Minimum account size: $ 2 Million
*(minimums may vary based upon product or whether account is
separately managed or commingled)*

Special areas of expertise:
Chancellor offers equity and fixed income investments
across the market capitalization spectrum. Equity
investments include large and small cap growth, core
(growth and value), market neutral and private equity.
Fixed income investments include full discretion,
enhanced cash, high yield and senior secured bank
loans. Combination products include balanced and
TAA portfolios.

Frequency of reporting results: Monthly

Assets managed by client category*:

	No. Clients MANAGED	Assets (in millions)
Corporate Funds	231	$14,200
Public Funds	37	4,700
Taft-Hartley Funds	15	600
Endowments & Foundations	54	900
Insurance	27	7,400

*As of 3/31/94

Investment approaches:
Chancellor believes that the highest quality investment management services can be provided to clients
through rigorous, repeatable processes. Our investment process is differentiated by a disciplined interplay of fundamental and quantitative resources. We
continually refine our investment processes to provide
consistently outstanding investment performance and
client service, tailored to the particular needs and
objectives of our clients.

Delaware Management Company, Inc.

One Commerce Square, Philadelphia, PA 19103

Key Contact Information:
Minette van Noppen
Vice President-National DC Sales Dir.   215-751-2910
Jerry Alrutz, *Vice President*   215-988-1669
Martin Cole, *Vice President*   215-988-1668

Year Founded: 1929

Organization: Delaware Management Company, Inc.
is a professional investment firm which serves as the
manager for the Delaware Group of mutual funds. In
addition to 55 years of mutual fund management,
Delaware has also provided individual portfolio, or "separate account" management for corporate and public
retirement plans since 1972. Delaware International
Advisers Ltd. was established in 1990 for the management of international equity and fixed income securities.

Total Assets Under Management:* $26 Billion

Assets by product type:*
Separately-Managed Accounts	$16.5 Billion
Mutual Funds	9.5 Billion

Assets by investment strategy:*
Cash/Other	$ 2.6 Billion
Fixed Income	4.4 Billion
Balanced	2.1 Billion
Conservative Equity	13.5 Billion
Aggressive Equity	1.8 Billion
International/Global	1.6 Billion

*As of 12/31/93

Service Approach: Nearly two-thirds of the assets
Delaware manages are attributable to retirement plans,
including those of some of the nation's largest corporations. Through these plans, Delaware manages the
retirement assets for approximately two million people.
Delaware's commitment to providing quality service
includes offering disciplined, long-term investment
strategies specifically suited to employee retirement
planning needs; investment management teams to
leverage professional expertise in portfolio decision-
making; mutual fund or individual portfolio structures
for maximum ongoing cost efficiencies; educationally-
oriented investment communications to improve
employee understanding; and simplified IRA programs
to accommodate direct rollovers.

The Dreyfus Trust Company
144 Glenn Curtiss Boulevard
Uniondale, NY 11556-0144

Key Contact Information:

Oliver St. C. Franklin *Sr. VP Sales-Public Funds*	212-922-8490
John E. Igneri *Sr. VP Sales-Corporations*	212-922-8420
William E. Martin, *VP Sales-Endowments, Foundations & Unions*	212-922-8436

Year Founded: 1984

Total Assets Under Management/Administration:
About $5 Billion

Special areas of expertise:
The Dreyfus Trust Company offers investment management services and products in a variety of investment disciplines, including: Small Cap, International Equity, International Recovery, Sector Rotation, Global and U.S. Fixed Income and Cash/Cash Equivalents.

Frequency of reporting results: Quarterly

Investment Approaches:

Small Cap: Fundamental, bottom-up investment style. Focus on companies with market cap below $750 million with dominant market positions, low-cost production, capital self-sufficiency and likelihood of benefitting from social/economic changes.

International Equity: Regional research teams cover international markets. Identify long-term value investments through rigorous bottom-up fundamental analysis combined with top-down economic, country and market research.

International Recovery: International returns can be enhanced through investing in the shares of companies experiencing difficulties, where we believe the market is undervaluing prospects for recovery. In searching for such deep value opportunities, market capitalization varies with small to medium companies dominant in the portfolio.

Sector Rotation: Large Company Growth, Large Company Value, Small Company Growth and Small Company Value.

Fixed Income: Value manager. Returns are enhanced through sector rotation and issue selection.

Fidelity Investments®
82 Devonshire Street, Boston, MA 02109

Key Contact Information:
Fidelity Institutional Retirement Services Company
(A division of Fidelity Investments Institutional Service Company, Inc)

Robert Reynolds, *President*	617-330-2888
Peter Smail, *Sr. Vice President*	617-330-0335

Fidelity Management Trust Company

Alexander Webb III, *President*	617-563-6677
Edward E. Madden, *Exec. V.P., Dir.*	617-563-6144

Year Founded: 1946

Assets Under Management:

	No. of Clients*	Assets*
Total FMR:	6M *shareholders*	$250 Billion
Total Retirement Services Company:	4000	$60 Billion
Total Management Trust Company:	196	$20.8 Billion

*as of 3/31/94

Special Areas of Expertise:
Fidelity Management & Research Company offers a range of mutual fund products to institutional and retail clients. Fidelity Management Trust Company provides separate account management and commingled pools to institutional investors through a range of investment disciplines.

Investment Approach: For all our disciplines, our investment philosophy is consistent with Fidelity's 48-year history.

Fundamental Research: We base decision-making on in-depth knowledge of companies and credits.

Adherence to Investment Disciplines: A consistent, well thought out investment discipline governs each portfolio's objectives, investment universe, buy and sell disciplines, desired characteristics and expected performance pattern.

Fully Invested Portfolios: Fidelity does not engage in market timing.

Portfolio Managers Have Responsibility and Accountability: Within their disciplines, portfolio managers have broad investment latitude and unlimited access to resources, and they are strictly accountable for performance.

Instinet Corporation

875 Third Avenue, New York, NY 10022
212-310-9500 • Fax: 212-838-8125

Key Contacts:
Davis Gaynes, *SVP Sales & Marketing*
Marc Gresack, *SVP International Sales & Trading*

Instinet Corporation provides global agency brokerage services to clients trading in over 30 countries on 5 continents. Instinet's strict neutrality ensures every client full anonymity, allowing institutions, broker-dealers and specialists to trade directly with each other on an equal footing. As a result, clients reduce the potential for market impact and frequently negotiate trades between the spread, reducing transaction costs. Instinet is registered with the U. S. Securities and Exchange Commission as a broker-dealer and is a member of the NASD. Affiliates of Instinet are members of: AMEX, U. S. Regional Exchanges, Chicago Board Options Exchange, Toronto Stock Exchange, London Stock Exchange, European Options Exchange (Amsterdam), Frankfurt Stock Exchange, Zurich Stock Exchange, the Paris Bourse and the Stock Exchange of Hong Kong.

Services:
- Equity trading in over thirty countries
- Trading in U. S. convertible bonds
- List trading for quantitative investors
- Real-time research and analytics
- Passive crossing services
- Soft and directed commission services
- Securities lending management

Offices:
New York, Toronto, London, Paris, Zurich, Frankfurt, Tokyo and Hong Kong

Mellon Trust

Retirement Services Group, One Mellon Bank Center, Suite 1445, Pittsburgh, PA 15258-0001
Fax: 412-234-9477

Year Founded:	1869

Key Contact Information:
Timothy F. Keaney,
Senior Vice President   412-234-1336
Allen R. Murray, *Vice President*   412-234-5507

Organization:
With the acquisition of the Boston Company in 1993, the combined portfolio of the two organizations represents more than $750 billion in institutional assets under trust and administration. The united organization, known as Mellon Trust, is one of the largest U.S. master trustees and the second largest U.S. global custodian of tax-exempt assets. In the 1993 Global Investor survey, plan sponsors rated Boston Safe Deposit and Trust, now a part of Mellon Trust, as the number one global custody service provider. Mellon has also agreed to merge with The Dreyfus Corporation, the sixth largest U.S. mutual fund company. The combined organization will meet growing demands for an array of high-quality financial products delivered by a single source.

Service approach:
Mellon's Retirement Services Group serves the defined contribution market, including 401(k), 457, and 403(b) plans. Mellon offers Participant Services, Plan Administration, Investment Management, Employee Communications, Recordkeeping, Benefit Disbursement, Trust & Custody, and Consulting/Technical Support — all that can be customized and bundled in any combination. A complete defined contribution package effectively meets the needs of today's more enlightened and demanding employee base.

Institutional Trust Clients by category:

	No. of Clients	Assets ($ millions)
Corporate Funds	405	$310,300
Public Funds	16	42,300
Unions (Taft-Hartley)	12	14
Foundations & Endowments	54	47,000
Other	116	350,400
Total	603	750,000

Merrill Lynch, Pierce, Fenner & Smith, Inc.

Key Contacts:
MERRILL LYNCH BUSINESS FINANCIAL SERVICES
Retirement and Employee Benefit Services

Rene M. Campis, *Director*, Large Market Sales and Client Service	609-282-3002
Barry M. Gross, *Director*, Retirement and Investment Services (small and mid-size markets)	609-282-2462
Donna M. Winn, *Director*, Marketing and Operations (large markets)	609-282-2233

Years in 401(k)/ Defined Contribution business:	20 years
Retirement plan assets:	$42 Billion
Number of plans served:	2,581
Number of plan participants:	1.25 Million
Frequency of valuation:	Daily

Special areas of expertise:
As an established leader in providing global financial services, Merrill Lynch has long been a leading provider of employee benefit plan programs, focusing our resources on developing services and products to meet the many financial needs of corporations and their employees.

Merrill Lynch has been successful in structuring flexible and dynamic 401(k) and other employee benefit plan services, including Employee Stock Purchase Plans, Employee Stock Option Plans, Deferred Compensation Plans, and our customized Corporate Savings Programs. Flexibility means choice, and Merrill Lynch provides plan sponsors with a menu of service selections, including a wide variety of investment options, recordkeeping and administrative support, employee communications and trust services.*

Merrill Lynch also recognizes the growing desire of employees to participate in planning their financial future. This evolving interest often generates the need for improved education to help employees define savings objectives and design investment strategies. Merrill Lynch can assist plan sponsors in customizing a sophisticated corporate benefits program to address employee needs.

*Trust Services are not available in all states.

MetLife
One Madison Ave., New York, NY 10010

Key Contacts:

Nicholas Latrenta, *Vice President*	212-578-3761
Gary Lineberry, *Vice President*	212-578-3181
Felix Schirripa, *Vice President*	212-578-6492

Total tax-exempt assets under management from all sources:	$77.5 Billion

Wholly-Owned Investment Management Subsidiaries: State Street Research & Management Company actively manages equity and fixed income assets for individual and institutional separate accounts and mutual funds. MetLife Investment Management Corporation (MIMCO) provides active fixed income management of diversified, mortgage-backed, asset-backed, private placement, and duration constrained portfolios for individual and commingled separate accounts. GFM International Investors, Ltd., London specializes in active non-U.S equity and fixed income management of separate account and mutual fund products.

Number of Clients (all sources):

Corporate Funds	1303
Public Funds	113
Unions (Taft-Hartley)	89
Foundations & Endowments	8

Investment Approaches:
State Street Research draws upon specialized internal research and "bottom-up" equity analysis. A "top-down" fixed-income philosophy utilizes interest rate forecasting, yield curve analysis, and duration constraints. MIMCO achieves incremental return to fixed income portfolios through duration management, sector weighting, issue selection, yield curve analysis, and interest rate anticipation with emphasis on credit and quantitative research. GFM's active management strategy includes country allocation, currency weighting, and issue selection. In the firm's core macroeconomic view, equity selections are based upon fundamental valuation methods, while fixed income issues are selected through the variation of interest rate exposure, yield curve analysis, and maturity structure.

NCM Capital Management Group, Inc.

103 West Main Street, Durham, NC 27701-3638
Phone: (919) 688-0620 • Fax: (919) 683-1352

Key Contact Information:
Maceo K. Sloan, CFA, *Chairman, President & CEO*
Justin F. Beckett, *Executive Vice President*
Clifford D. Mpare, CFA, *Senior Vice President*
Mary M. Ford, *Vice President*
Marc V. Reid, *Asst. Vice President*

Year founded: 1986

**Total tax-exempt assets under
management from all sources:** over $2.5 Billion

Minimum account size: $10 Million (separate)
$1 Million (commingled)

Special areas of expertise:
Equity, fixed income, and balanced portfolio management emphasizing low-risk fundamentals.

Frequency of reporting results:
Monthly, Quarterly, Annually (per client request)

Assets managed by client category:

	No. of Clients	Assets Managed (in millions)
Corporate funds	16	$ 708
Public funds	33	1,537
Unions (Taft-Hartley)	14	218
Foundations & Endowments	9	73.5

Investment Approach:
NCM Capital's equity philosophy is *value* oriented, employing a quantitative methodology to identify stocks with low relative and absolute price earnings ratios. We analyze positive earnings surprise and attractive earnings momentum relative to all other stocks in our universe. NCM Capital's fixed income philosophy is *quality* oriented, recognizing that most investors will assume duration risk, but prefer insulation from the extreme price volatility of low-quality fixed income securities. Portfolios are invested in high-grade securities and managed within client-defined investment objectives and risk parameters.

Index to Underwriters

ANNOTATED BIBLIOGRAPHY

I. RECOMMENDATIONS FROM THE AUTHORS

NATHANIEL DUFFIELD:

"Seismic Shift in Pension Planning," Greenwich Associates. 1994 Investment Management Survey. Greenwich, CT, 1994. *This annual survey is an excellent overview of general trends among both DB and DC plans.*

Investment Policy: How to Win the Loser's Game by Charles D. Ellis (Homewood, IL: Dow Jones-Irwin, 1985). *This book, one of six by Greenwich Associates's Ellis, contains valuable insights for anyone involved in formulating investment policy.*

Asset Allocation by Roger C. Gibson (Homewood, IL: Dow Jones-Irwin,1990). *Gibson addresses this critical aspect of the investment process substantively, without getting overly technical.*

The Investor's Guide to Emerging Markets by Mark Mobius (London: Pitman Publishing, 1994). *Mobius heads emerging markets equity management at the Templeton Funds, one of the original, most successful players in this market. The author travels throughout the markets he covers; his book is an excellent source of information and opinion.*

Guaranteed Investment Contracts: Risk Analysis and Portfolio Strategies by Kenneth L. Walker (Homewood, IL: Dow Jones-Irwin, 1989). *An authoritative volume for fiduciaries involved in buying and managing GIC portfolios.*

Managing Your Investment Manager: The Complete Guide to Selection, Measurement and Control by Arthur Williams III (Homewood, IL: Dow Jones-Irwin, 1986). *A hard-to-find, hands-on, practical guide to managing managers.*

SALLY GOTTLIEB:

Employee Benefit Programs: A Total Compensation Perspective by Robert M. McCaffery (Boston, MA: PWS-KENT Publishing Company, 1992, Second Edition). *An excellent overview of employee benefits and how they meet employee needs, it describes the pros and cons of various plan designs and includes a lucid comparison of DB and DC plans.*

Fundamentals of Employee Benefit Programs (Washington D.C.: Employee Benefit Research Institute, 1990, Fourth Edition). *In addition to describing basic design options, this valuable reference addresses administrative issues and legal constraints.*

Employee Benefits Handbook by Jeffrey D. Mamorsky (Boston, MA: Warren, Gorham & Lamont, 1992, Third Edition). *An excellent reference (updated annually) that covers design options, applicable laws and regulations and more. A must for every benefits administrator.*

The Pension Benefits Answer Book by Stephen J. Krass (Boston, MA: Warren, Gorham & Lamont, 1992). *A follow-up to the* **Employee Benefits Handbook** *with even more detail on plan design, laws and regulations.*

"The Changing Profile of Pensions." Employee Benefit Research Institute. Washington, DC, 1985. *Thought-provoking insights on the history, evolution and future trends of pension plans.*

RITA METRAS:

The 401(k) Plan Management Handbook by Jeffrey M. Miller (Chicago, IL: Probus Publishing Company, 1993). *This guide for establishing and overseeing 401(k) plans features informative sections on fiduciary responsibility and investment policy.*

Selecting Investments for Your Retirement Accounts by Richard D. Glass, Ph.D., CEBS (Pittsburgh, PA: Investment Horizons, Inc. 1993). *This 85-page, easy-to-read handbook is designed to help plan participants make informed investment decisions.*

The Investor's Encyclopedia by Chet Currier and the Associated Press (New York, NY: Franklin Watts, Inc., 1987). *Although targeted for the individual investor, this book provides a good overview of investments and their risks, rewards, costs and liquidity.*

"The Annual Survey of Profit Sharing and 401(k) Plans." Profit Sharing Council of America. Chicago, IL. *See listing under "Organizations."*

"401(k) Plan Hot Topics." Hewitt Associates. Lincolnshire, IL, 1993.

"Retirement Planning in America: Do Plan Sponsors and Participants Agree on the Important Issues?" Frank Russell Company. Tacoma, WA, 1992.

II. RECOMMENDATIONS FROM THE EDITORS

OVERVIEW

ERISA Fiduciary Answer Book by Rory Judd Albert, Esq., Jacob I. Friedman, Esq. and Neal S. Schelberg, Esq. (New York, NY: Aspen Publishers, 1994). *This exhaustive tome includes legal definitions, regulations, case histories, checklists and Q&A for sponsors and fiduciaries.*

404(C) REFERENCES

"A Guide to Complying with ERISA 404(c)," Proskauer Rose Goetz & Mendelsohn. New York, NY, 1993.

How ERISA Section 404(c) Affects You and Your Firm's Retirement Savings Plan by Luke D. Bailey, Esq. and Dale W. Shultz, PFP (Emeryville, CA: Shultz, 1993). *A clear concise guide to understanding 404(c) in the larger context of ERISA; includes definitions and interpretations of fiduciary liability.*

"Now That the 404(c) Regulations are Final, Who Cares?" by Robert Eccles and David Gordon. ERISA Litigation Reporter, Vol. I, No. 11 (December 1992): pp. 15-23.

"Final Regulation Regarding Participant Directed Individual Account Plans (ERISA Section 404(c)) Plans," Pension & Welfare Benefits Administration, U.S. Department of Labor, 29 CFR Part 2550, Federal Register, Vol. 57, No. 198, October 13, 1992. *The final 404(c) rule. The document includes comments received by the DOL which affected the final regulation.*

401(K) RESOURCES

The 401(k) Provider Directory by David Huntley and Joseph Valletta (Towson, MD, 1993). *Designed for plan sponsors, this directory covers types of plans, services and service providers, and fee information. Includes worksheets to help plan sponsors comparison-shop. (410) 296-1086.*

"The Personal 401(k) Adviser," issued by the Institute of Management Administrators. *A new newsletter for plan sponsors and service providers. Perry Patterson, Group Publisher (212) 244-0360.*

"Defined Contribution News," published by Institutional Investor, Inc. *This semi-monthly newsletter covers who's doing what, regulation trends, products, hires and fires in the DC industry. It is probably the best overall source of news in the DC world.*

GLOSSARY

Call Option: A contract which gives the right to buy a specified number of shares of a security (stock or bonds), or units of a foreign currency or stock index, at a pre-determined price (strike price) within a given deadline in exchange for a premium. The buyer expects that the future price of the security will be lower than the strike price. A "put" option grants the right to sell a given number of securities.

Out-of-the-Money Call: An option whose exercise price is higher than the current value of the underlying security.

Guaranteed Investment Contract: A contract issued by a bank or life insurance company which guarantees the invested principal plus a fixed interest accumulation at a set maturity date. If the issuing company fails, investors have recourse only to the insurer's general account, as do all other creditors.

Index Fund: A passively managed portfolio of stocks or bonds which seeks to replicate the performance of the corresponding market index, such as the S&P 500 or the Shearson/Lehman Government bond index.

Separate Account (GIC): An investment account actively managed by a life insurance company on behalf of a particular investor or group of investors. Assets within this account are held and invested solely for the investor's benefit and are not subject to claim by other creditors. Should the issuer fail, the investor has rightful claim to the assets in the underlying portfolio (although practically speaking, this could take time). Thus, the portfolio is "wrapped" within the contract. Separate accounts, like synthetic GICs, were created in the early 1990s in response to losses suffered by GIC holders following such insurance company failures as that of Executive Life.

Soft Dollars (also called **Directed Commissions** or **Commission Recapture**): A form of payment used by money managers for investment research and related services bought through brokerage commissions generated through trades. Only offered by specific third-party brokers.

Standard Deviation: A measure of the mathematical deviation from the mean of two-thirds of a statistical sample. For example, if the average annual return on the stocks of the S&P 500 were +15%, and the standard deviation was +/- 15%, two-thirds of the time the return of any stock chosen at random would fall between 0% and +30%. Standard deviation reflects the unpredictability of returns and is a useful indicator of risk.

Synthetic GIC: A contract packaged and guaranteed by a bank or life insurance company supported by an underlying portfolio of securities managed by an outside investment manager. Unlike a separate account GIC, the securities may be held by the plan sponsor's custodian. A complex instrument, the synthetic GIC offers more credit and market diversification than the traditional GIC without credit risk (if the issuer fails, the investor retains the assets). Another advantage is book value accounting. Synthetics don't require market-to-market accounting, thus volatility is smoothed out over the life of the portfolio.

Unitized Accounting: Accounting for ownership interest in a pool of assets by issuing units of participation value based on the net value of the asset pool. Sub-unitized accounting involves unitizing assets contained in an already unitized pool; for example, accounting for a pure equity fund from equities actually held within a balanced fund whose assets are already unitized for holders.

AUTHORS' BIOGRAPHIES

Nathaniel H. Duffield joined the Dallas-based Halliburton Company in 1983 as Director - Trust Investments. He is responsible for the day-to-day management and investment of the company's $3.5 billion worldwide retirement plan, one of the earliest, most innovative DC plans. As an investment professional, he is atypical among DC plan sponsors in his capacity as Chairman of Halliburton's Trust Investment Committee. Previously, Duffield was Director of Employee Benefit Funds for E-Systems. His lifelong career in the defense and energy sectors has given him expertise in dealing with erratic corporate financial results and their implications for pension investing.

Duffield holds a B.B.A. in Finance from the University of Oklahoma and graduated from the Southwestern Graduate School of Banking at Southern Methodist University. He is a member of the Committee on the Investment of Employee Benefit Assets (CIEBA) of the Financial Executives Institute; the GIC Association; the Dallas/Fort Worth Metroplex Pension Sponsors Group; and the Interforum Plan Sponsor Group for Foreign Pension Plans.

Sally Gottlieb, Benefits Manager, Apple Computer, Inc. in Cupertino, California, oversees plan design and administration, employee communications and legal compliance for Apple's domestic benefit programs. She also manages their Records group which supervises data integrity and systems changes for the company's employee database. Before joining Apple in 1989, Gottlieb was part of the pension investment group at Pacific Gas & Electric Company where she administered the company's DB and DC plans. At both Apple and PG&E Gottlieb played an important role in two major plan conversions. Her experiences in two different, equally volatile industries, helped develop her belief that benefits policy must be aligned with overall corporate strategy.

A graduate of the University of California at Berkeley, Gottlieb has been an instructor of the American Compensation Association's since 1983. She is a member of the San Francisco chapter of the Western Pension Conference and belongs to the Silicon Valley Compensation and Benefits Association.

Rita D. Metras has been Director, Employee Benefits – Retirement and Savings Plans at the Eastman Kodak Company in Rochester, New York since 1991. Under her tenure the $3.8 billion DC plan began to evolve from primarily a savings vehicle into an integral part of the total retirement benefit. In conjunction with the treasurer's staff, Rita's department began a large-scale expansion of plan offerings which culminated in three new fund additions in February 1994. Previously, she played a key role in implementing additional investment options in the plans of two Kodak subsidiaries.

Metras joined the benefits department in 1988 after serving for 18 years in a variety of capacities in human resources and marketing information systems. In June 1994, she was appointed Director of Benefits Strategy – Welfare Plans.

The Vice Chairman of the Profit Sharing Council of America, Metras also teaches benefits courses for the American Compensation Association. She holds a B.A. in Mathematics from the College of St. Elizabeth and a master's degree from the Rochester Institute of Technology.

THE BUILDING BLOCKS OF CREATIVE FINANCE

ITEX corporation is a dynamic nationwide business-to-business barter company in one of the country's most important growth industries. In the U.S. alone, business barter now represents a $7 billion industry growing in excess of 15% a year.

Corporations, governments and not-for-profits share the common need and goal of reducing operating costs. Shaving a few basis points is not the only way. More and more organizations use barter as an alternative to cash for business transactions.

After twelve years in operation. ITEX is the established leader in giving smart money managers opportunities to use business-to-business barter.

For more information contact
Martin Kagan, Vice President
ITEX corporation
One Lincoln Center - Box 2309
Portland, OR 97208-2309
Phone 503 244 4673
Fax 503 245 0748

Traded on NASD
Bulletinboard
Symbol: ITXE

OTHER 1994 INVESTORS PRESS INVESTMENT MANAGEMENT BOOKS

THE CHANGING FACE OF PENSION MANAGEMENT:
Rescripting the Role of Plan Sponsors, Trustees, Money Managers and Consultants

May 1994

FILLING THE VACUUM:
Alternative Investments for Pension Plans, Endowments and Foundations

October 1994

ARGENTINA TO ZIMBABWE:
A Global Allocator's Guide to Evaluating Emerging Markets

December 1994

COPIES OF **A WING AND A PRAYER** ARE AVAILABLE FOR $35 EACH INCLUDING TAX, HANDLING AND SHIPPING COSTS. PLEASE ALLOW THREE WEEKS FOR DELIVERY. PLEASE SPECIFY QUANTITY AND OTHER TITLES YOU ARE ORDERING. PAYMENT AND MAILING INSTRUCTIONS SHOULD BE MAILED TO:

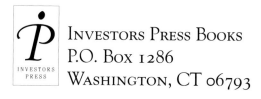

INVESTORS PRESS BOOKS
P.O. BOX 1286
WASHINGTON, CT 06793